Chess Opening Workbook for Kids

Graham Burgess

CHOOSE BETWEEN...

GAMBIT

First published in the UK by Gambit Publications Ltd 2020
Reprinted 2022

ISBN-13: 978-1-911465-37-9
ISBN-10: 1-911465-37-6

DISTRIBUTION:
Worldwide (except USA): Central Books Ltd, 50 Freshwater Road, Chadwell Heath, London RM8 1RX, England.
Tel +44 (0)20 8986 4854 Fax +44 (0)20 8533 5821. E-mail: orders@Centralbooks.com

Gambit Publications Ltd, 27 Queens Pine, Bracknell, Berks, RG12 0TL, England.
E-mail: info@gambitbooks.com
Website (regularly updated): www.gambitbooks.com

Edited by Graham Burgess
Typeset by Petra Nunn
All illustrations by Shane Mercer
Printed and bound by TJ Books, Padstow, Cornwall, England

10 9 8 7 6 5 4 3 2

Gambit Publications Ltd
Directors: Dr John Nunn GM, Murray Chandler GM, and Graham Burgess FM
German Editor: Petra Nunn WFM
Bookkeeper: Andrea Burgess

Contents

Chess Notation

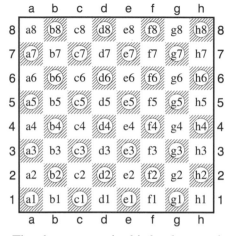

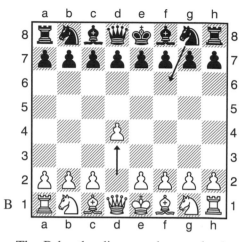

The chess moves in this book are written in the standard chess *notation* that is in use throughout the world. It can be learned by anyone in just a few minutes.

As you can see from the left-hand chessboard above, the vertical columns of squares (called *files*) are labelled a-h and the horizontal rows of squares (called *ranks*) are numbered 1-8. This gives each square its own unique name. The pieces are shown as follows:

Knight =   ♘
Bishop =   ♗
Rook =   ♖
Queen =   ♕
King =   ♔

Pawns are not given a symbol. When they move, only the *destination square* is given.

In the right-hand diagram above, White has already played the move **1 d4**. The **1** indicates the move-number, and **d4** the destination square of the white pawn. Black is about to reply **1...♘f6** (moving his knight to the **f6-square** on his *first move*).

The B by the diagram shows who is to move. The following symbols are also used:

Check	=	+
Double check	=	++
Capture	=	x
Checkmate	=	#
Castles kingside	=	0-0
Castles queenside	=	0-0-0
Good move	=	!
Bad move	=	?
Interesting idea	=	!?
Not recommended	=	?!
Brilliant move	=	!!
Disastrous move	=	??

To check you've got the hang of it, play through the following moves on your chessboard: 1 e4 c6 (this opening is called the Caro-Kann) 2 d4 d5 3 ♘c3 dxe4 (the pawn from the *d*-file captures on e4) 4 ♘xe4 ♘d7 5 ♗c4 ♘gf6 (the knight on the *g*-file moves to f6) 6 ♘g5 e6 7 ♕e2 h6?? (a very bad move). You should now have reached the position shown in Exercise 9 on page 8.

Introduction

Are you looking to start your chess games more purposefully? To get your pieces on great squares and give your opponents immediate problems? To be ready to pounce when they make mistakes? Then this is the book for you!

But you will not be taught these things like in a classroom. You will learn them for yourself by tackling exercises featuring a wide range of opening themes. This way you will remember the ideas far better and develop the problem-solving skills you need to win chess games.

This format means that tactics are dominant in most of the exercises. When you've worked out an answer, you'll want to know if it is right or wrong, rather than read an essay about some subtle differences between your options! But I've also worked as many strategic points as I can into the solutions, explaining what strategic errors allowed the tactic, or which goals of opening play were relevant. And the later chapters of the book address key areas of opening strategy: you are often challenged to find the best way to attack the centre or to exploit poor development or a failure to castle. More about that on page 84.

Back to basics. I am assuming that you know how to play chess, have played at least a few games and are familiar with basic tactical ideas. If you have finished the first book in this series, John Nunn's *Chess Tactics Workbook for Kids*, then you are more than ready. Some knowledge of chess openings is useful, but not essential. I'll sometimes refer to named openings, but you don't have to know any names to enjoy this book. An understanding of opening *principles* will definitely make these exercises easier to solve. Many of the ideas seen in my own work *Chess Opening Traps for Kids* reappear in this book.

Think carefully about each position before making your decision or answering the question. In a real game you get no second chances, so for this to be useful training, you need to treat it in the same way. Please study each solution carefully, especially if you didn't get the right answer. All that matters is what you learn, so don't get dispirited! Bear in mind that later exercises often feature themes from earlier ones, so you may get a chance to use your new knowledge sooner than you expect. It will be sweetest to spring these ideas to win real games, of course.

Feel free to set up the diagram positions on a chessboard. But when I refer to a move in the diagram caption, *do not make this move on your board!* Why not? Because some ideas are easy to see when you have the position right in front of you, but actually need to be seen a move or two earlier. This is the skill you are developing in those exercises.

Towards the end of each chapter, especially later in the book, the exercises become rather difficult. If they are beyond you, don't worry. You can come back and study them later, or just read the solutions and learn everything you can from them. At the end of the book comes a short chapter with the hardest positions in the book, followed by a series of tests that help you measure your skill.

So please dive in, enjoy the book, and then wow the world with your amazing opening play!

1 Warn-Ups

When you have played the opening well, and your opponent has not, it might be possible to win the game with a clear-cut tactic. Always be alert, or you might miss your chance!

In this first chapter I present a small selection of such positions. In many cases, they are simpler versions of ideas we see in later chapters. So don't skip this chapter, even if it looks too basic for you. Solving these positions will help fix the ideas in your mind and make them easier to find later in the book – or in real games – when there is more going on to distract you.

In our first position above, White has a neat way to win, but it is very easy to miss. After 7 exf7+ Black must play 7...♚e7 (since 7...♚xf7 8 ♕xd8 picks off his queen), and then comes a neat promotion trick: 8 fxg8♘+!! (8 fxg8♕? lets Black save his queen by 8...♕xd1+ 9 ♚xd1 ♖xg8) 8...♖xg8 (8...♚e8 9 ♕h5+) 9 ♗g5+ and the black queen is lost. Does this look familiar? It is the reverse of a well-known trap in the Albin Counter-Gambit (1 d4 d5 2 c4 e5). But spotting that it is the same idea with the board position reversed is quite tricky.

In the second position, do you think you might be tempted to play 5...d5? It seems like a good way to attack White's pawn-centre, as Black uses his fast development to attack the e4-pawn. If so, you would have fallen for a nasty tactic, as 5...d5?? allows the queen fork 6 ♕a4+, which wins a piece. But there is another important point to make here. Even though Black has allowed a simple tactic, White must still play carefully. After 6...♘c6 (otherwise White plays 7 ♕xb4), it is most accurate to reply 7 cxd5! exd5 8 ♗b5, winning the knight cleanly. Instead both 7 exd5?! b5! and 7 ♕xc6+ ♗d7 8 ♕b7 ♘xe4 give Black more play than was necessary.

- Avoid choosing an 'obvious' move without thinking first. Imagine the position *after* the move and check for tactics.
- Make good use of your 'mental database' of chess ideas. A familiar pattern might be there, but in some altered form.

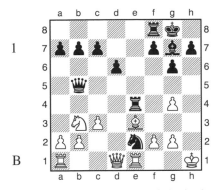

1

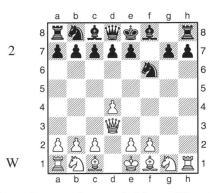

2

White believed the black knight had to retreat. What had he missed?

Open lines and a weak king... How does White win?

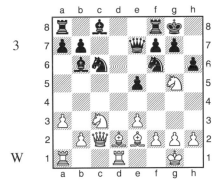

3

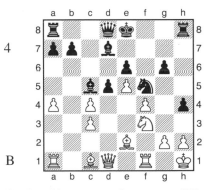

4

Must White retreat his attacked knight?

White has his eyes on the centre. Where is Black looking?

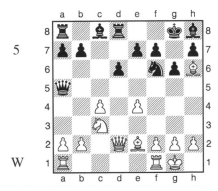

5

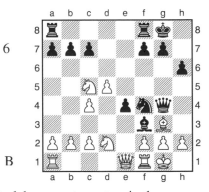

6

The black king is short of squares. How do you take advantage of that?

Black has a neat way to win the game on the spot.

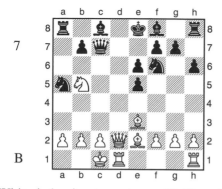

7 B

White is hoping to mate on d8. How does Black focus attention on the white king?

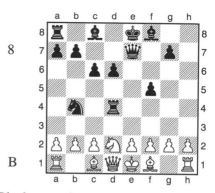

8 B

"Black can play 13...f4, ignoring White's pawn fork with 14 c3." True or false?

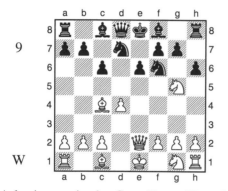

9 W

A basic trap in the Caro-Kann. How does White win?

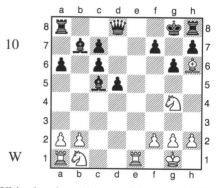

10 W

White has just given up his queen. Why?

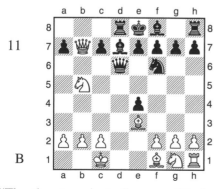

11 B

"The threat against c7 means Black must give up his queen." True or false?

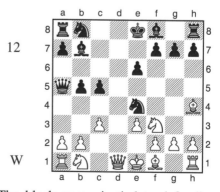

12 W

The black queen is tied to defending d8. How do you take advantage of that?

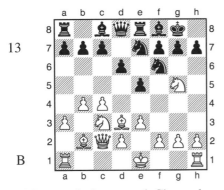

13

B

The h7-pawn is threatened. Choose between 10...h6 and 10...g6.

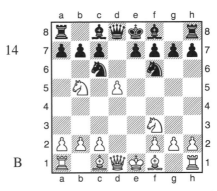

14

B

White has just played 7 d5. Why doesn't this move simply lose a pawn?

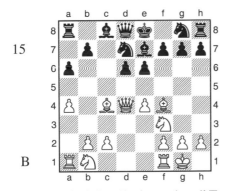

15

B

"The pawn fork 8...e5 wins a piece." True or false?

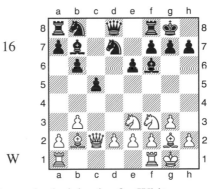

16

W

A standard trick wins for White.

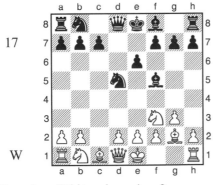

17

W

How does White win a piece?

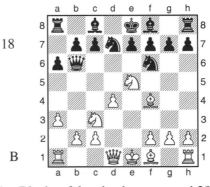

18

B

Can Black safely take the pawn on b2?

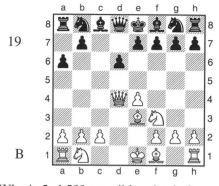

19 B

Why is 5...b5?? a terrible mistake?

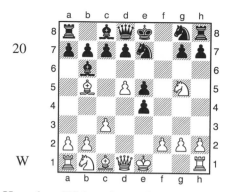

20 W

How does White win on the spot?

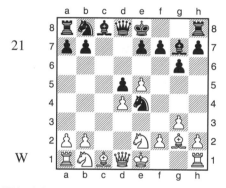

21 W

"Black has powerfully centralized his knight."
True or false?

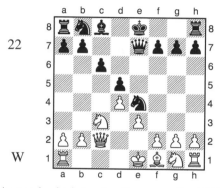

22 W

A standard trick wins the game for White.

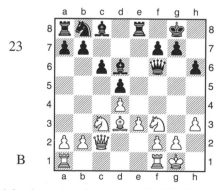

23 B

A basic tactic wins a pawn for Black. What is
it?

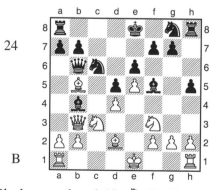

24 B

Black now played 10...♞e7. What had he
overlooked?

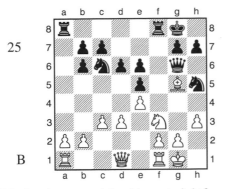

25

B

Black wins material with a straightforward tactic.

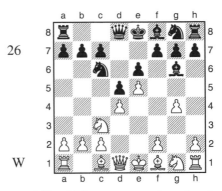

26

W

Now 6 ♘ge2? is a very careless developing move. Why?

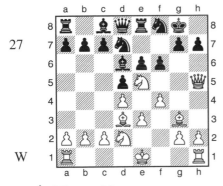

27

W

Does ♗xh7+ work?

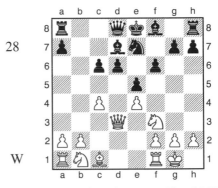

28

W

The pawn on d6 looks tasty. Should White take it?

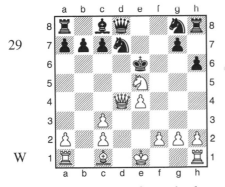

29

W

King-hunt! How do you force checkmate?

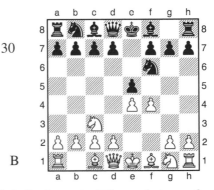

30

B

Fight for the centre! Choose between 3...♗b4 and 3...d5.

Solutions to Warm-Up Exercises

1) Black forces mate with 17...♕h5+!! 18 gxh5 ♖h4#, a pattern known as Anastasia's Mate.

2) 6 ♖xh7! demolishes Black's flimsy defences since if he takes the rook, White replies with 7 ♕g6#.

3) 16 ♘d5! wins – this is the basic theme of an idea called the Siberian Trap normally used by Black, though it is a little harder to recognize with colours reversed and some of the pieces on different squares. 16...♘xd5 allows 17 ♕h7#, and otherwise Black loses his queen.

4) At the h-file and White's king! 16...♘g3+! wins: 17 hxg3 hxg3+ and mate next move.

5) 13 ♘d5! wins instantly. 13...♕xd2 14 ♘xe7# is mate and otherwise Black loses his queen.

6) 17...♕h3!! forces mate. 18...♕xg2# is threatened, and 18 gxh3 ♘xh3# is a beautiful mate with the minor pieces.

7) 13...♘b3+! wins: 14 axb3 ♖a1# is mate, while 14 ♔b1 ♘xd2+ is check, so leaves Black a queen up.

8) True. After 13...f4, 14 c3?? blunders into an instant smothered mate thanks to the pin on the e-file: 14...♘d3#.

9) 8 ♘xf7! ♔xf7 (now it's mate in three, but otherwise Black loses a lot of material) 9 ♕xe6+ ♔g6 10 ♗d3+ ♔h5 11 ♕h3#.

10) Because he now mates with 18 ♖e8+! ♗f8 (or 18...♕xe8 19 ♘f6#) 19 ♖xf8+ ♕xf8 20 ♘f6#.

11) Well, sort of true, since the best reply *is* to sacrifice the queen... but to force mate in three: 11...♕d1+! 12 ♔xd1 ♗g4++ 13 ♔e1 (or 13 ♔c1 ♖d1#) 13...♖d1#.

12) 9 ♗xb5+! wins a pawn since 9...♕xb5? allows 10 ♕d8#.

13) I hope this was an easy choice because 10...h6?? allows mate in two by 11 ♗h7+ ♔h8 (11...♘xh7 12 ♕xh7#) 12 ♘xf7#! Nevertheless, this type of mate is missed surprisingly often in practice, especially when calculating ahead a few moves. Instead, 10...g6 is a solid move with no particular drawbacks.

14) 7...♕xd5?? clearly loses the queen because of the knight fork 8 ♘xc7+. What might be less obvious is that 7...♘xd5?? fails because of the same theme: 8 ♕xd5! ♕xd5 9 ♘xc7+ and White emerges a piece up.

15) False. 8...e5?? is a terrible mistake since 9 ♕d5 leaves Black unable to defend f7. After 9...♘h6 10 ♗xh6 0-0 11 ♗e3 it is White who has won a piece.

16) 13 ♘g5! is a decisive double attack on h7 and b7. After 13...♗xg5 14 ♗xb7 White wins a full piece, while 13...♗xg2 allows 14 ♕xh7#.

17) With a one-two punch by pawn and queen: the pawn fork 6 e4! lures the bishop to e4 and then 6...♗xe4 7 ♕a4+ forks king and bishop.

18) No, because after 8...♕xb2?? 9 ♘a4! the queen is trapped.

19) 5...b5?? lets White trap the rook in the corner with 6 ♕d5. After 6...♕c7 7 ♕xa8 ♘c6 Black is nowhere near able to trap the queen.

20) 8 ♘e6! traps the black queen because the d7-pawn is pinned.

21) That might be true if the white knight were on f3 instead of e2, but all he has done here is get the knight trapped in the middle of the board. After 9 f3 ♕a5+ the fact that the king can sidestep with 10 ♔f1 seals the knight's fate.

22) 9 ♘xd5! wins material thanks to the pin on the c-file. 9...cxd5 (there's nothing better, as otherwise Black loses his queen or his e4-knight) 10 ♕xc8+ ♕d8 11 ♗b5+ and White will win comfortably.

23) 12...♗xh3! picks off a pawn in front of White's king because 13 gxh3 leaves the f3-knight unprotected: 13...♕xf3.

24) He had missed that 10...♘e7?? loses to 11 ♕xb4 because of the pin on the c6-knight. This is a surprisingly common type of error, even among strong and experienced players, even though everyone knows that a pinned piece does not defend.

25) 14...♖xf3! removes the defender of the g5-bishop, so after 15 ♕xf3 ♕xg5 Black has two knights for a rook and should win.

26) 6 ♘ge2?? loses because after the simple 6...♘b4! White has no way to defend c2 and loses heavy material. He can't even save his rook by 7 ♖b1? because 7...♗xc2 8 ♕d2 ♘d3+ wins the queen, and 7 ♔d2 ♗xc2 8 ♕e1 ♘d3 is similar.

27) Yes. 11 ♗xh7+! forces a neat mate in fact: 11...♘xh7 12 ♕f7+ ♔h8 13 ♘g6#.

28) No, 10 ♕xd6?? is a terrible mistake because 10...♘d5! traps the queen. However, Black has put his pieces on some odd squares to set this little trap, and simple play with 10 ♘c3 intending ♖d1 and ♗e3 gives White an excellent game.

29) There are plenty of strong options for White, but a clear-cut forced mate with all checks should not be missed: 11 ♕d5+! ♔f6 (or 11...♔e7 12 ♕f7+ ♔d6 13 ♘c4+ ♔c6 14 ♕d5#) 12 ♕f7+ ♔xe5 13 ♗f4+ ♔xe4 14 f3#.

30) 3...♗b4? is a plausible-looking move that pretty much loses! Black seeks to remove the knight that controls e4, but the problem is that after 4 fxe5! ♗xc3 5 dxc3! ♘xe4 (5...♘g8 6 ♘f3 is simply terrible for Black) 6 ♕g4! the knight is unsupported and 6...d5 (or 6...♘c5 7 ♕xg7 ♕h4+ 8 ♔d1) 7 ♕xg7 ♖f8 8 ♗h6 is game over. 3...d5! is correct, and gives Black a very satisfactory game. A standard continuation is 4 fxe5 ♘xe4 5 ♘f3 ♗e7 6 ♕e2 ♘xc3 7 dxc3 c5, when Black controls a lot of the centre and has no bad pieces.

WARM-UPS

2 Mate

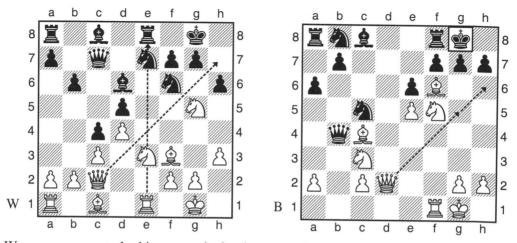

We now move on to looking at particular themes, and start with the most important of all: checkmate! The king starts the game poorly defended, with few pieces in place to protect him. Mate threats can be created within just a few moves. In some positions in this chapter there is a clear-cut mate to be found, but more often you need to find a good move (or avoid a bad one) where a mating idea is important, but not absolutely forced.

Our first diagram offers a good example. Black has just played 16...h6??, ruining an excellent position. Why is that? The pin on the e-file allows White to play 17 ♘xd5!!, a modified form of the Siberian Trap, an idea we saw in the previous chapter. 17...♘fxd5 allows mate by 18 ♕h7+ ♔f8 19 ♕h8+ ♘g8 20 ♘h7#, while 17...♗f5 18 ♘xc7 ♗xc2 19 ♘xe8 leaves Black hopelessly down on material, and 17...♘exd5 18 ♖xe8+ ♘xe8 19 ♕h7+ ♔f8 20 ♗xd5 gives White a decisive attack.

When under attack, it is important to identify all of the opponent's mating ideas. In our second diagram, White has the obvious threat of ♕g5 intending ♕xg7#. Seeing this, Black might choose 17...♘e4??. However, this loses because White has a further and less obvious mating idea: 18 ♕h6!!, with the point 18...gxh6 19 ♘xh6# (another theme from Chapter 1). Therefore Black needs a way to deal with both threats. It's tricky, but if you know what you are looking for, you have a better chance of finding it! The answer is 17...exf5!, since after 18 ♕g5 ♘e6 19 ♗xe6, Black parries the threats by 19...♕g4!, keeping a decisive material advantage.

- Don't just do "I go there, he goes there" analysis. Take a look at the whole position. Do you see any familiar patterns? Do you see ideas that might work if a piece were on a different square, or not there at all? Can you make those things come true with a sacrifice? Be bold!
- Active pieces and weaknesses? There are likely to be several threats.
- If you can get three pieces around the enemy king, there is a good chance there will be a mate. Two may be enough if the king is poorly defended.
- 'Defenders' can also get in the way of a king by blocking its escape routes.

14

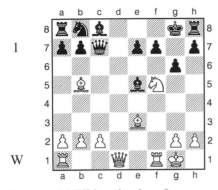

1

What should White play here?

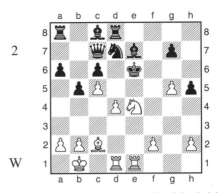

2

How would you checkmate the black king?

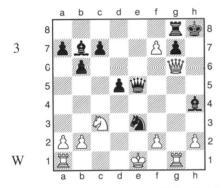

3

A wild position! How does White finish the game?

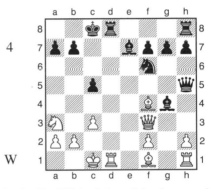

4

It looks like White is horribly skewered. But in fact he can win the game on the spot.

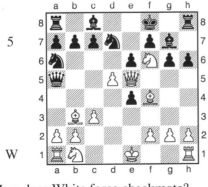

5

How does White force checkmate?

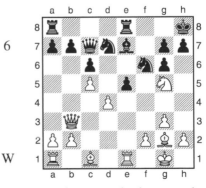

6

Force mate using a standard pattern that you have surely seen before.

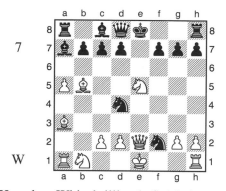

7

How does White brilliantly finish the game?

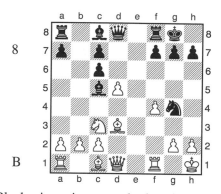

8

Black wins using a standard mating pattern.

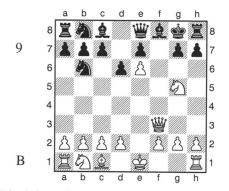

9

Black is a piece up, but has only one good move here. What is it?

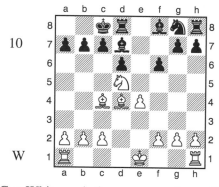

10

Can White grab the pawn on a7 or will his bishop be trapped?

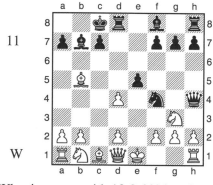

11

What is wrong with 12 0-0?? here?

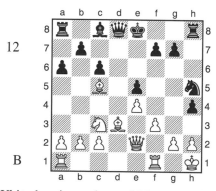

12

White has just taken a bishop on c5. How does Black reply?

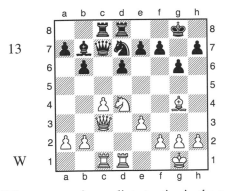

13

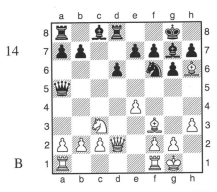

14

"There are no immediate tactics in the position." True or false?

Should Black avoid the exchange of bishops with 13...♗h8 here?

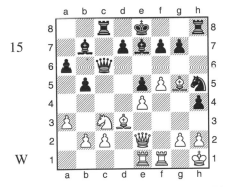

15

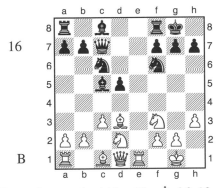

16

Should White exchange bishops on e7?

Does the standard idea 11...♗xh3 12 gxh3 ♕g3+ work here?

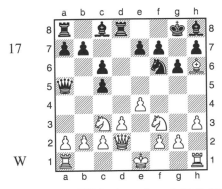

17

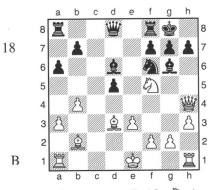

18

In two games White has played 11 0-0 here. What is he threatening then?

Black is under pressure. Is 18...♘e4 a good way to free his game?

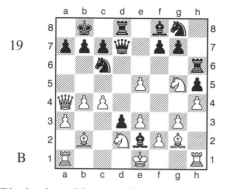

19

B

Black wins with a surprising twist on an idea we have seen before.

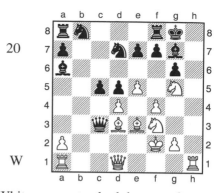

20

W

White uses a standard theme to force mate.

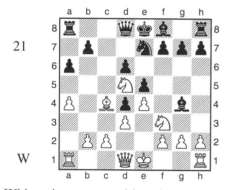

21

W

White wins a pawn with a nice tactic, based on mate.

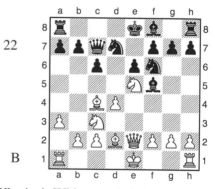

22

B

Why isn't White worried about Black grabbing a pawn with 10...♗xc2 here?

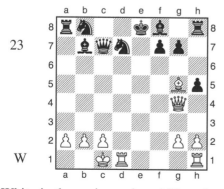

23

W

White is three pieces down! How does he win?

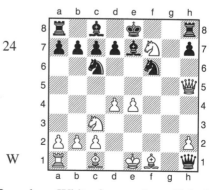

24

W

How does White force a beautiful checkmate?

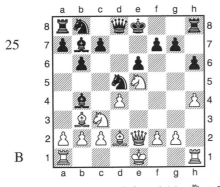

25

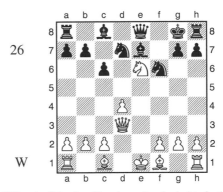

26

Choose between 11...0-0 and 11...♘xc3.

Why is Black allowing the knight fork 11 ♘c7 here?

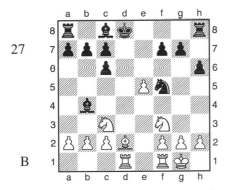

27

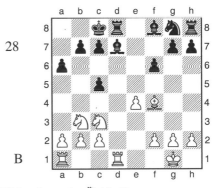

28

Black innocently exchanged on c3 with 11...♗xc3. What happened next?

White intends ♘d5. Do you prevent that with 11...c6 or 11...♗e6 here?

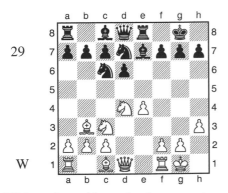

29

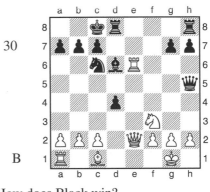

30

White wins with a classic queen-trapping theme.

How does Black win?

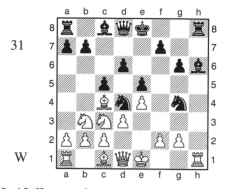

31

Is 13 f3 a good way to push Black's pieces back?

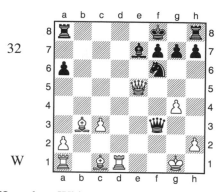

32

How does White round off the game before Black develops his rooks?

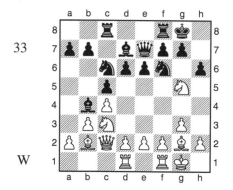

33

Familiar themes can pop up in unexpected places. What do you see here?

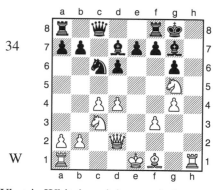

34

What is White's quickest and cleanest way to win the game?

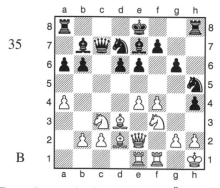

35

Does the standard sacrifice 17...♘g3+, blasting open the h-file, work here?

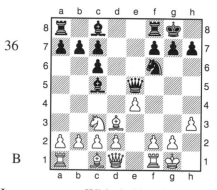

36

How secure are White's kingside defences?

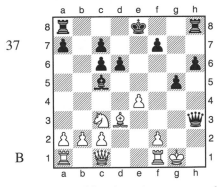

37

B

Black has sacrificed a piece to attack the white king. But what is his follow-up idea?

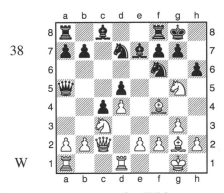

38

W

Do you see any way for White to snatch a pawn?

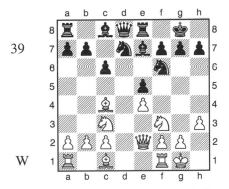

39

W

Black has just put his rook on e8. Do you spot a big weakness? What do you play?

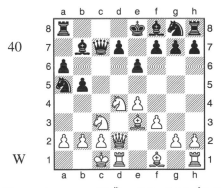

40

W

Choose between 10 ♘xe6 fxe6 11 ♗b6 and 10 ♘dxb5 axb5 11 ♘xb5.

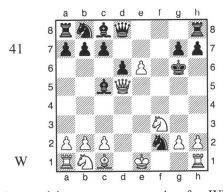

41

W

A surprising pawn move wins for White. Which one?

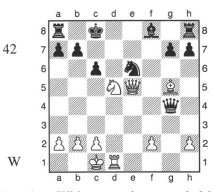

42

W

How does White mate the uncastled black king?

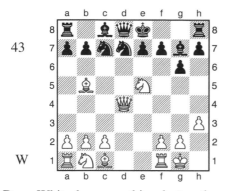

43

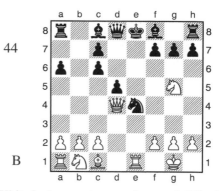

44

Does White have anything better than exchanging lots of pieces on d7?

White is threatening to take on e4. Why isn't 9...♕f6 a good defence against that?

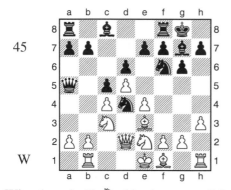

45

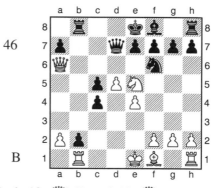

46

Why doesn't 11 ♘xd4 win a pawn? Is 11 ♖d1 a good way to prepare this?

Both 12...♕b5? and 12...♕b7? are losing moves. Why?

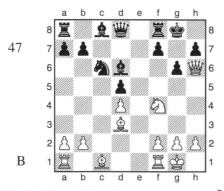

47

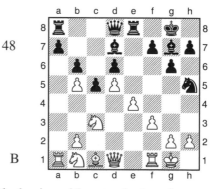

48

Black defended the d5-pawn with 13...♘e7. What happened next?

Black wins with a standard tactic.

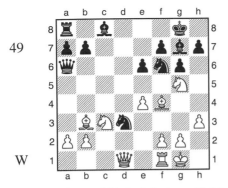

49

Black has plunged his knight into d3, hitting f4 and b2. How should White reply?

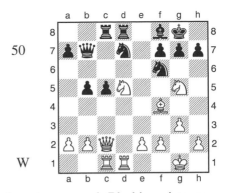

50

A neat move ends Black's resistance.

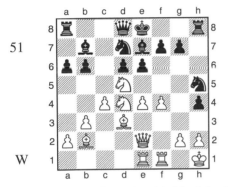

51

"White smashed through with 16 e5 dxe5 17 ♘xe6 and mate followed." True or false?

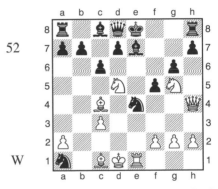

52

White finds a spectacular way to win, based on double checks and mate.

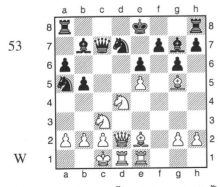

53

White opted for 16 ♘dxb5 axb5 17 ♘xb5. Was this a good idea?

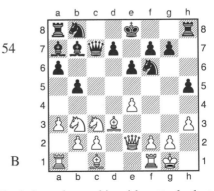

54

Black launches a kingside attack that is a typical idea in this opening structure.

Solutions to Mate Exercises

1) It's mate in two: 15 ♘h6+! ♚g7 (15...♚f8 16 ♖xf7#) 16 ♖xf7#.

2) 21 ♘d6+! ♘e5 (or 21...♚d5 22 ♗b3#) and now White has a choice of ways to mate in two moves, including 22 ♗f5+ ♚d5 23 ♖xe5#.

3) He forces mate with 20 ♕h6+! gxh6 21 fxg8♕#.

4) 14 ♕c6+!! bxc6 15 ♗a6# is a well-known mating pattern called Boden's Mate. Instead 14 ♘b5?? threatens mate, but loses to 14...♖xd1+.

5) 17 ♕d6+!! cxd6 18 ♗xd6# is a very neat way to mate a king.

6) 16 ♘f7+! ♚g8 17 ♘h6++ ♚h8 (17...♚f8 18 ♕f7#) 18 ♕g8+! leads to a 'Philidor's Legacy' smothered mate, since no black piece is covering the f7-square: 18...♖xg8 19 ♘f7# or 18...♘xg8 19 ♘f7#.

7) With mate in two based on a double check: 12 ♘xd7+!! ♘xe2 13 ♘f6#.

8) 12...♕h4! (not 12...♘xh2?? 13 ♕h5) 13 h3 and now 13...♕g3! threatens mate on h2, forcing White to capture on g4, which opens the h-file: 14 hxg4 ♕h4#.

9) 8...h6?? allows a surprising mate: 9 ♕f7+ ♕xf7 10 exf7#. But after 8...g6! there is no mate, and Black will play ...♗g7, ...♘c6 (and maybe ...h6) and win thanks to his extra material.

10) 11 ♗xa7! wins a pawn for nothing, since 11...b6? (a standard idea to trap a bishop in positions like this) walks into 12 ♗a6#. Look out for this idea after queenside castling!

11) 12 0-0?? loses to the spectacular 12...♕h3!!, when 13 gxh3 ♘xh3# is a beautiful mate with the two minor pieces.

12) 13...♘g3+! leads to a standard mating pattern: 14 hxg3 hxg3+ 15 ♚g1 ♖h1+ (15...♕h4 followed by ...♕h1# is actually a move quicker, but a foolproof mate with checks is never bad) 16 ♚xh1 ♕h4+ 17 ♚g1 ♕h2#. White could play on with two pieces for a queen after 14 ♚g1, but it is hopeless.

13) False. Black's weakened kingside allows a typical tactic: 18 ♘e6! (threatening ♘xc7 and ♕g7#) 18...fxe6 19 ♗xe6+ ♚f8 20 ♕h8#.

14) Definitely not. 13...♖h8?? loses to 14 ♘d5!, when ♕xa5 and ♘xe7# are both threatened, so Black is either mated or loses his queen. The bishop exchange is not a problem for Black in any case, who has a good position after 13...♗e6 (e.g., 14 ♘d5 ♕xd2, when 15 ♘xe7+?? ♚f8 costs White a piece) or 13...♗xh6 14 ♕xh6 ♗e6.

15) If you were working out what happens after 17 ♗xe7 ♘xe7 18 ♘d5+, then you had missed something important! 17 ♗xe7?? is a blunder because Black replies 17...♘g3+!, winning the queen or mating after 18 hxg3 hxg3+ 19 ♚g1 ♖h1+ 20 ♚xh1 ♕h6+ 21 ♚g1 ♕h2#.

16) Yes, it does. 11...♗xh3! 12 gxh3? (this loses, but otherwise White has lost a good pawn for nothing) 12...♕g3+ 13 ♚h1 ♕xh3+ gave Black a winning attack in a girls under-10 event because 14 ♘h2 ♕xd3 costs White the bishop on d3. After 14 ♚g1 the neatest win is 14...♗xf2+! 15 ♚xf2 ♘g4+, forcing a quick mate.

17) 11 0-0 threatens the deadly ♘d5!, winning the black queen due to the ♘xe7# idea. One game ended 11...♘d7?? 12 ♘d5! 1-0. Note that the immediate 11 ♘d5?? loses a piece because 11...♕xd2+ is check.

18) No, because 18...♘e4?? loses to 19 ♕h6! gxh6 20 ♘xh6#.

19) 14...♘d4! uncovers an attack on the white queen, and since 15 ♕xd7 allows 15...♘c2#, there's no time to save her majesty. Be extra careful when your king has no safe squares.

20) 18 ♖h8+!! both frees a square for the queen *and* forces the king or bishop to a worse square. 18...♗xh8 (or 18...♔xh8 19 ♕h1+ ♔g8 20 ♕h7#) 19 ♕h1 and Black can't avoid mate since 19...♖c8 is met by 20 ♕h7+ ♔f8 21 ♕xh8# thanks to the bishop having been decoyed to h8.

21) 10 ♘xe5! has the main point that 10...♗xd1? 11 ♘f6+ gxf6 12 ♗xf7# is mate, so after 10...dxe5 11 ♕xg4 White is a pawn up.

22) Because 10...♗xc2?? allows a deadly standard sacrifice: 11 ♘xf7! ♔xf7 (11...♖g8 12 ♘g5 followed by taking on e6 is hopeless for Black) 12 ♕xe6+ ♔g6 13 ♕f7+ ♔f5 14 ♗e6#.

23) 18 ♕e2+! (not 18 ♖he1+?? ♘e5 19 ♖xe5+ ♗e7, when the king slips away) 18...♘e5 (or 18...♕e5 19 ♕xe5+ ♘xe5 20 ♖d8#) 19 ♕xe5+! ♕xe5 (19...♕e7 20 ♗xe7 ♗xe7 21 ♖he1 is hopeless for Black, as is 19...♗e7 20 ♕xc7 ♗xg5+ 21 ♔b1) 20 ♖d8#.

24) With a modified form of Philidor's Legacy: 12 ♘d6++! ♔d8 (12...♔f8 13 ♕f7#) 13 ♕e8+ and now 13...♘xe8 14 ♘f7# or 13...♖xe8 14 ♘f7#. The black pieces on c8 and c7 act like the edge of the board in the familiar version of this mate in the corner.

25) 11...♘xc3?? is a blunder because after 12 bxc3! ♗e7 (12...♗d6 13 ♘xf7! is similar) 13 ♘xf7! ♔xf7 Black will be mated: 14 ♕xe6+ ♔e8 15 ♕g6+ ♔d7 16 ♗e6+ ♔d6 17 ♗f4+, etc. So 11...0-0 is the best option (e.g., 12 ♘xd5 ♗xd2+), as it avoids opening the b3-bishop's diagonal. Black will come under attack on the kingside, but can certainly hope to defend.

26) He is not worried about 11 ♘c7? because he has a sneaky answer up his sleeve: the double check 11...♗b4++! forces mate: 12 ♔d1 ♕e1#.

27) The problem with 11...♗xc3?? is that White does not recapture, but instead checkmates with 12 ♗g5++ ♔e8 13 ♖d8#. Never assume your opponent will automatically recapture a piece!

28) 11...c6?? is a terrible mistake because it allows the knight to use a different route with devastating effect: 12 ♘a4! threatens instant mate, and there is no good answer because 12...b5 13 ♘b6+ picks off the d7-bishop. 11...♗e6 is a solid move that gives Black a playable game; e.g., 12 ♘d5 ♖d7 or 12 ♖xd8+ ♔xd8 13 ♖d1+ ♔c8 14 ♘d5 ♗xd5 15 ♖xd5 b6.

29) 10 ♗xf7+! ♔xf7 11 ♘e6! ♔xe6 (otherwise the queen is lost for just two pieces) 12 ♕d5+ ♔f6 13 ♕f5#.

30) 13...d3! is a similar idea to the Siberian Trap. The pawn-thrust clears a square for the black knight to overload its white cousin on f3. 14 ♕xd3 loses to 14...♗xh2+, while after 14 ♕e4 and 14 ♕e3 both 14...♘d4 and 14...dxc2 are winning. The main point is 14 cxd3 ♘d4! 15 ♕e4 (15 ♘xd4 ♕xh2+ 16 ♔f1 ♕h1#) 15...♘xf3+ 16 gxf3 ♕xh2+ 17 ♔f1 ♗c5, when White is defenceless; e.g., 18 ♗e3 ♗xe3 19 ♕xe3 ♕h1+ and ...♕xa1.

31) No, 13 f3?? is a terrible mistake because of 13...♗d2+! 14 ♔xd2 (14 ♕xd2 ♖xh1#) 14...♕g5+ and ...♖xh1# is coming. White should instead complete his development after making a couple of exchanges: 13 ♗xh6 ♖xh6 14 ♖xh6 ♘xh6 15 ♕d2 and 0-0-0, with a good position.

32) 22 ♕xe7+! drags the black king into a crossfire. After 22...♔xe7 23 ♗a3+ ♔e8 24 ♗a4+ ♘d7 25 ♗xd7+ ♔d8 26 ♗c6+ White regains the queen and will be two bishops up.

33) It's another version of the Siberian Trap! After 12 ♘d5! the only way to avoid mate or loss of the queen is 12...exd5 but White's last move opened the way for the bishop, and 13 ♗xf6 eliminates the key defender. So Black loses king or queen in any case.

34) 15 ♖h8+! forces a quick mate: 15...♗xh8 (or 15...♔xh8 16 ♕h2+ ♔g8 17 ♕h7#) 16 ♕h2 ♔g7 (16...♗xd4 allows 17 ♕h7#, while after 16...♖e8 17 ♕h7+ ♔f8 White even has a choice of mates) 17 ♕h7+ and the great escape with 17...♔f6 doesn't get very far: 18 ♘ce4#.

35) Yes, it does. After 17...♘g3+! 18 hxg3 hxg3+ 19 ♔g1 the check 19...♕c5+! brings the queen quickly to the h-file: 20 ♘d4 (trying to decoy the queen, but it has another path to the h-file; 20 ♗e3 ♕h5 and ...♕h1# follows) 20...♕xd4+ 21 ♕e3 ♖h1+! 22 ♔xh1 ♕h8+ 23 ♔g1 ♕h2#.

36) Not secure at all, as 9...♗xh3! shatters them. After 10 gxh3 ♕g3+ the queen invades thanks to the pin on the f2-pawn, and following 11 ♔h1 ♕xh3+ 12 ♔g1 ♘g4 it will soon be mate. And 10 ♕f3 ♗g4 leaves the queen trapped since 11 ♕g3 ♕xg3 exploits the pin again.

37) With 17...g4! Black intends simply ...g3 and ...♕h2#, and there is very little White can do to stop it. 18 ♘e2 g3 19 ♘xg3 is no help because of 19...♕xg3+ (pin!) 20 ♔h1 ♕h3+ 21 ♔g1 ♖g8+, mating.

38) 13 ♘xd5! is yet another form of the Siberian Trap. It doesn't attack the black queen as usual, but the loose bishop on e7 provides the second weakness. Black loses at least a pawn since 13...♘xd5?? 14 ♕h7# is the standard mate, while 13...hxg5? 14 ♘xe7+ ♔h8 is simply awful for Black.

39) 10 ♗xf7+! ♔xf7 11 ♕c4+ launches a winning attack: 11...♔f8 12 ♘g5 and with ♕f7# and ♘e6+ both threats, the game is over. 11...♘d5 12 exd5 ♘b6 13 ♕e4 is terrible for Black, while 11...♔g6 allows a king-hunt. After 12 ♘h4+ ♔h5 13 ♕e2+ ♔xh4 the neatest way to mate is 14 ♔h2 followed by 15 g3#. Instead 10 ♘g5? misses the chance, because 10...♖f8 defends comfortably.

40) Both are tempting and standard ideas, but one of them is very bad in this precise position. 10 ♘dxb5? axb5 11 ♘xb5?? loses because of 11...♘b3+! 12 axb3 ♖a1#, while 10 ♘xe6!! fxe6 (or 10...dxe6 11 ♗b6!) 11 ♗b6! (followed by ♗xa5) wins a pawn with a great position since 11...♕xb6? allows 12 ♕xd7#.

41) After 9 g4! there's no answer to the threats of ♕f5# and ♕h5+. After 9...♖f8 10 ♕h5+ ♔f6 11 ♗g5+ the black queen is lost, while 9...♘xg4 gives up the e4-square so 10 ♕e4+ ♔h5 11 ♕f5+ g5 12 h4 forces mate. Other moves in the diagram position don't work: 9 h4? h6 lets the king escape, while 9 b4? ♕f6 costs White the e6-pawn and with it any hope.

42) By blocking a flight square and opening the d-file. That sounds quite mundane when put into words, but the moves themselves are highly dramatic: 20 ♕c7+! ♘xc7 21 ♘b6+! ♔b8 (21...axb6 22 ♖d8#) 22 ♖d8+ ♘c8 23 ♖xc8# (or even 23 ♘d7#).

43) Yes, he does. 11 ♘xd7! is a decisive queen sacrifice, since 11...♗xd4 (11...♗xd7 12 ♕xg7 is hopeless for Black) 12 ♘f6++ ♔f8 13 ♗h6# is mate because the knight has cut off the bishop's retreat from d4.

44) 9...♕f6?? is answered anyway with 10 ♘xe4! because 10...♕xd4 allows mate by 11 ♘f6++ ♔d8 12 ♖e8#, and 10...dxe4 11 ♕xe4+ ♗e7 12 ♗g5! ♕xg5 (12...♕e6 13 ♗xe7) 13 ♕xc6+ is hopeless for Black. The best option for Black in the diagram position is 9...♗e6.

26

45) The problem with 11 ♘xd4?! cxd4 12 ♗xd4 is 12...♘xe4! 13 ♘xe4 ♕xd2+ 14 ♔xd2 ♗xd4, regaining the pawn with a good position. 11 ♖d1?? does threaten to win a pawn, but falls foul of 11...♘xe4! because 12 ♘xe4 ♘c2# is mate since the rook has taken the last flight square from the king and the queen is pinned.

46) Both queen moves lose because of a skewer plus some mating ideas: 12...♕b5? 13 ♖xb2! ♕xb2 (13...♕xa6 14 ♖xb8+ and mate next move) 14 ♕c6+ ♔d8 15 ♘xf7#. 12...♕b7? 13 ♖xb2! is basically the same, as 13...♕c7 14 ♖xb8+ ♕xb8 15 ♕c6+ leads to mate next move.

47) After 13...♘e7?? White executed his main idea: 14 ♘h5!, threatening ♕g7#, and meeting 14...gxh5 with 15 ♕xh7#. 14...♘f5 15 ♗xf5 removes the defender, and 14...♗xh2+ 15 ♔h1 changes nothing. Never assume your opponent has only one threat: here the f4-knight had far more sinister intentions than grabbing the d5-pawn.

48) 16...♗d4+! exploits the white king's lack of room and exposure on the dark squares. The move f3 firmly supports the e4-pawn but means great care must be taken with the king. 17 ♔h1 (17 ♖f2 avoids mate but loses material) 17...♘g3+! 18 hxg3 ♖e5 and a deadly check follows on the h-file since the only way to stop ...♖h5+ is 19 g4 (19 f4 ♖h5+ 20 ♕xh5 gxh5 isn't enough for the queen), which allows 19...♕h4#.

49) With 18 ♗c2! White is hunting for bigger game: his queen's entrance on d8 will create havoc. The variations are not complex, but the idea is easy to miss because of the instinct to respond to an attack on a piece before considering other options. 18...♘xf4 (18...h6 19 ♗xd3 hits the queen, and so wins a piece) 19 ♕d8+ ♗f8 20 ♕xf6 and Black will be mated. He would have no way to defend f7, even if his knight weren't also under attack. Black's undeveloped queenside proved fatal here.

50) 18 ♗e5!! is a clever twist on the Siberian Trap theme. The bishop is immune because of 18...♘xe5 19 ♘xf6+ gxf6 20 ♕xh7#, while 18...g6 simply loses the knight on f6. Otherwise White is threatening 19 ♗xf6 ♘xf6 20 ♘xf6+ gxf6 21 ♕xh7#, and the final point is that 18...h6 19 ♗xf6! hxg5 20 ♗xd8 exploits the unfortunate placing of the black rook.

51) True, but only because the mate is by Black! After 16 e5?! dxe5 17 ♘xe6?? Black has the standard idea 17...♘g3+! 18 hxg3 (otherwise White loses his queen) 18...hxg3+ 19 ♔g1 ♗c5+! 20 ♘xc5 ♖h1+ 21 ♔xh1 ♕h4+ 22 ♔g1 ♕h2#. Always spare a thought for the opponent's ideas.

52) 15 ♘xe4! (15 ♖xe4?! fxe4 16 ♕f4 ♖f8 17 ♘c7+ ♕xc7 18 ♕xc7 is good for White, but far less clear) 15...♗xh4 (or: 15...fxe4 16 ♕xe4 cxd5 17 ♕xd5 ♖f8 18 ♗g5; 15...cxd5 16 ♘d6+ ♔f8 17 ♗h6+ ♔g8 18 ♗xd5#) 16 ♘d6+ ♔f8 17 ♗h6+ ♔g8 18 ♘f6#.

53) No, because after 16 ♘dxb5?? axb5 17 ♘xb5?? Black wins on the spot with 17...♘b3+! since the c2-pawn is pinned and 18 axb3 allows 18...♖a1#. 16 ♗xb5! is the right way to play this same idea, as after 16...axb5 17 ♘dxb5 ♕c6 18 ♘d6+ ♔f8 19 ♕f4 White wins.

54) The point behind 12...♘g4! is that an open h-file will be fatal for the white king with the black pieces raking down the three diagonals leading to f2, g2 and h2. 13 hxg4 (this loses, but 13 c5 gives away a pawn for nothing: 13...♘xe5!? 14 hxg4? ♕g3!) 13...hxg4 14 e5 and now the most elegant way to win is 14...♗f3! (14...f5 is good too) 15 gxf3 (15 ♕e1 ♕d8! intending ...♕h4 and ...♕h1#) 15...♕d8!, mating; e.g., 16 fxg4 (16 ♔g2 ♕h4 17 ♖g1 ♕h3#) 16...♕h4 17 ♔g2 (17 ♕f3 ♕h2#) 17...♕h3+ 18 ♔g1 ♕h1#.

27

3 Double Attack

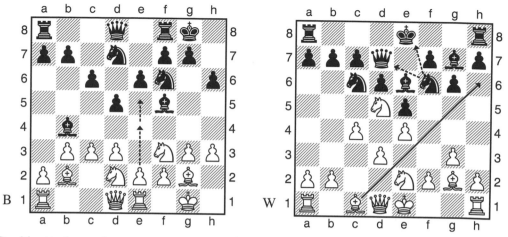

Double attacks are the most common type of chess tactic. The idea is simple: one move creates two threats. The opponent has only one move to deal with them, which may be impossible. Even if it is possible, he may be forced to play a move that sets him up for further problems.

In the opening, both players are scrambling to bring their pieces to good squares, and this will normally mean that some of them are unprotected for a while. You may only get a brief chance to attack these loose pieces, so be on the alert! Of course, if attacked by a *pawn*, a piece is in danger whether it is defended or not. Our first diagram above shows a pawn fork in action (when a single piece makes a double attack, it is called a *fork*). The b4-bishop is attacked and must choose a retreat. The obvious squares are d6 and e7. However, 11...♗d6?? loses a piece because of 12 e4 dxe4 13 dxe4 ♗h7 14 e5, forking bishop and knight. White's very modest set-up in the diagram position perhaps made it harder to spot this idea. Instead 11...♗e7 gives Black a fully acceptable position. If White now advances his e-pawn, he will not win a piece and a black knight may later find a nice square on d3.

In the second diagram it is all piece-play. White wins material with a typical opening tactic: 9 ♗h6! overloads the black bishop by exploiting the possible knight fork on f6. It is surprising that Black has no good answer at all. The main point is 9...♗xh6 10 ♘xf6+ (forking king and queen), while 9...♘xd5 10 ♗xg7 ♖g8 11 exd5 ♖xg7 12 dxc6 leaves White a piece up, 9...♔f8 allows 10 ♘xf6 thanks to the pin, and 9...♘h5 10 ♗xg7 ♘xg7 11 ♘f6+ is the fork again. After 9...0-0 10 ♘xf6+ ♗xf6 11 ♗xf8 White has won rook for bishop. This tactical idea occurs in several openings and can be used by White and Black.

- As with mate, thinking in terms of 'What if...?' is very useful in finding double attacks.
- Which enemy pieces are undefended? Can any be attacked by pawns?
- In the opening, knight forks are the most common type of double attack.
- The next best piece for double attacks in the opening is the queen. But check that the queen won't be *trapped* after your raid – much more about this in the next chapter!

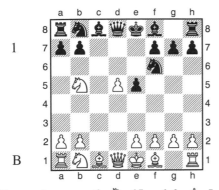

1

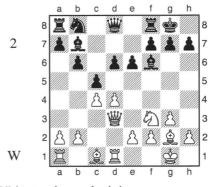

2

Choose between 6...♘xd5 and 6...♗c5.

White to play and win!

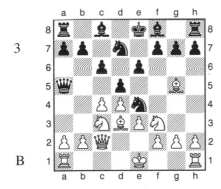

3

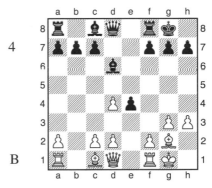

4

How does Black win a piece?

White's structure looks odd, but how bad are things?

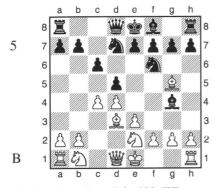

5

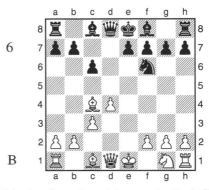

6

White has just played 6 c4??. Why was that a blunder?

White has just played the sneaky 7 c3. What is he planning if Black replies 7...♗f5?

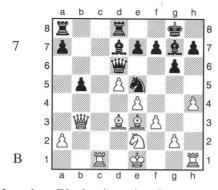

7

B

How does Black win a piece?

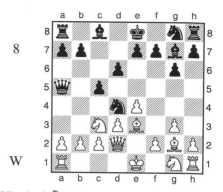

8

W

Why is 8 ♘h3?? a terrible mistake here?

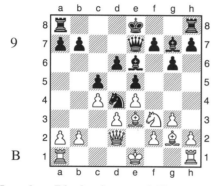

9

B

How does Black win material?

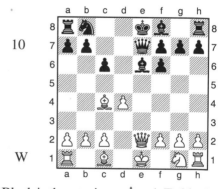

10

W

Black is threatening ...♗xc4. To block the e-file, White played 8 ♗e3. Was this good?

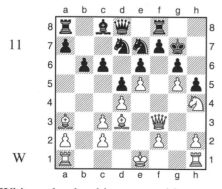

11

W

White unleashes his pawns with a very surprising move.

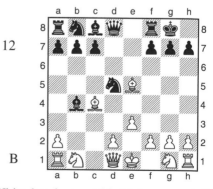

12

B

White has just put his bishop on c4. Black now cleverly wins a pawn.

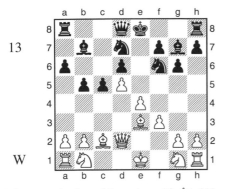

13

What standard problem does 13 ♗h6?? walk into?

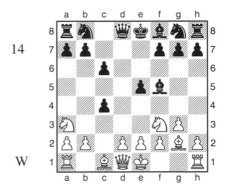

14

Should White take the pawn on e5?

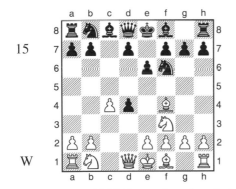

15

What happens if White makes the obvious recapture 5 ♘xd4 here?

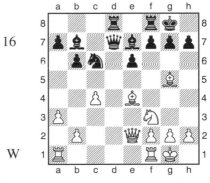

16

Which black piece is overworked?

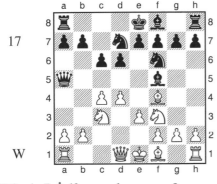

17

Why is 7 ♗d3 a careless move?

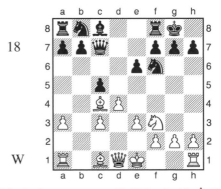

18

Black threatens ...cxd4. Why is 10 ♗d3 the wrong reply?

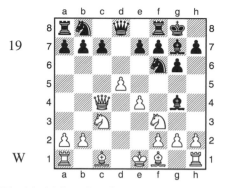

19 W

Black's bishop has just moved to g4. What happens next?

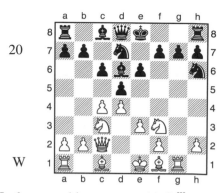

20 W

Is there anything wrong with 9 ♖xg7 here?

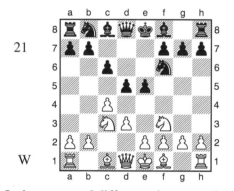

21 W

Is there any real difference between playing 5 cxd5 cxd5 6 ♘xe5 and 5 ♘xe5 here?

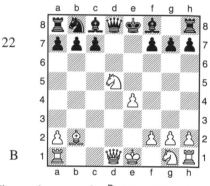

22 B

Choose between 8...♘d7 and 8...c6.

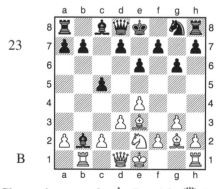

23 B

Choose between 9...♗g7 and 9...♕a5+.

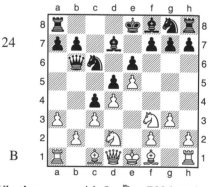

24 B

What's wrong with 8...♘ge7?? here?

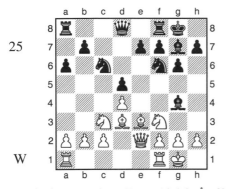

25 W

The pin is annoying. Does 12 h3 ♗xf3 13 ♕xf3 solve White's problems?

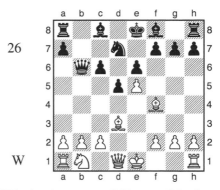

26 W

"Black wins a pawn." True or false?

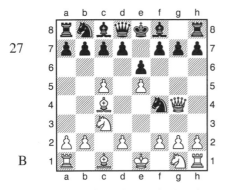

27 B

A knight-fork trick gives Black a huge advantage. But how and where?

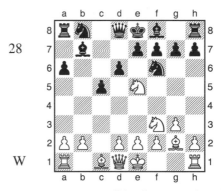

28 W

Do you see any possible discovered or double attacks?

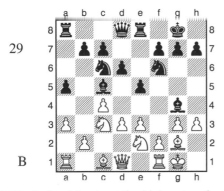

29 B

"Black should retreat the bishop to e6, planning ...d5, when he will have no problems." True or false?

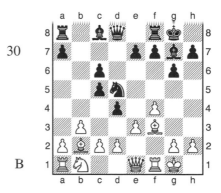

30 B

Neither 11...dxe3 nor 11...d3 achieves anything at present. Can you make them stronger ideas?

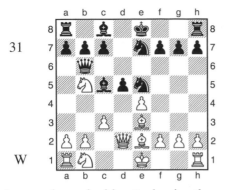

31

A very clever double attack wins the game for White.

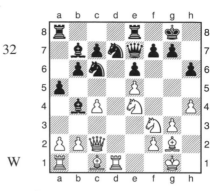

32

White finds a nice combination based on a knight fork.

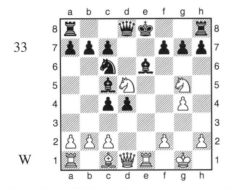

33

How does White unleash the power of his knights?

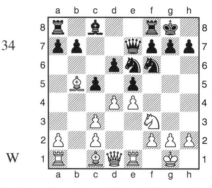

34

Black has just played 11...c5. Does this blunder the pawn on e5?

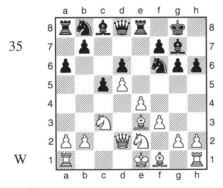

35

"12 ♗xh6 is strongly answered by the standard tactic 12...♘xe4!." True or false?

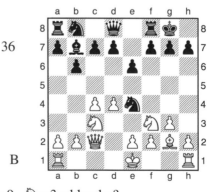

36

Is 9...♘xc3 a blunder?

Solutions to Double Attack Exercises

1) This should have been an easy choice since 6...♞xd5?? loses a piece because of the knight fork after 7 ♕xd5! ♕xd5 8 ♘c7+. So Black can't regain his pawn immediately. 6...♝c5! is Black's best option, developing quickly and looking to attack.

2) 12 ♘g5! wins with a standard double attack against b7 and h7: 12...♝xg2 allows 13 ♕xh7#, while 12...♝xg5 13 ♗xb7 traps the rook in the corner, winning material.

3) This is one of the classic traps in the Cambridge Springs, which has claimed countless victims in club-level chess around the world: 8...♘xg5! 9 ♘xg5 dxc4 and the double attack on the white bishop and g5-knight wins a piece for Black.

4) Black wins a key pawn thanks to a queen fork: 11...♝xg3! 12 fxg3? ♕xd4+ and ...♕xa1.

5) The problem is similar to the Cambridge Springs Trap: 6...dxc4! wins a piece. After 7 ♗xc4 ♕a5+ the queen check picks up the loose bishop. This has even cropped up at super-grandmaster level. The other key point is that White can't unload his bishop by 7 ♗xf6 because 7...cxd3 leaves two white pieces attacked.

6) 7...♝f5? would be a mistake because 8 ♕b3! is a simple but very effective double attack on b7 and f7. White wins a pawn and shatters Black's queenside pawns.

7) 16...♕b4+! decoys the white queen into a fork after 17 ♕xb4 (17 ♖c3 ♘xd3+ exploits a pin, while otherwise Black exchanges queens on b3 and wins the bishop on d3 in any case; e.g., 17 ♗d2 ♕xb3 18 axb3 ♘xd3) 17...♘xd3 and 18...♘xb4 with an extra bishop.

8) 8 ♘h3?? loses because 8...♝xh3! deflects the bishop from covering f3, so 9 ♗xh3 ♘f3+ delivers a deadly knight fork. 9 ♗xd4 doesn't save White since 9...cxd4 attacks the knight on c3.

9) 11...♝h3! is a standard tactic, deflecting the bishop to set up a fork. After 12 0-0 (12 ♗xh3? ♘xf3+ costs White his queen, while 12 ♘xd4? ♝xg2 followed by ...exd4 leaves Black a bishop up) 12...♘xf3+ 13 ♗xf3 ♝xf1 Black emerges with a rook for a bishop.

10) No. While 8 ♝e3?? breaks the pin on the e-file, it allows the double attack 8...♕b4+!, winning the white bishop.

11) 13 ♕f6+! ♘xf6 (otherwise Black loses the knight on e7) 14 gxf6+ ♚h7 15 fxe7 and not only has this lucky pawn taken two knights, but it now forks queen and rook, and threatens to promote! White emerges at least two pieces up.

12) 7...♘xe3! has the point that the d2-pawn is pinned, and 8 fxe3 allows the queen fork 8...♕h4+, winning the bishop on c4. 8 ♗xf7+? desperately seeks to avoid coming out a pawn down, but leads to bigger losses after 8...♖xf7 9 fxe3 ♕h4+ 10 ♝g3 (10 g3 ♕e4 traps the *other* rook!) 10...♕f6, winning the rook on a1.

13) 13 ♝h6?? loses a pawn because of 13...♘xe4! 14 ♗xe4 ♕h4+, winning back the piece with a huge advantage thanks to the fork by the queen.

14) No. 6 ♘xe5?? loses because of a theme we saw in *Chess Openings for Kids*: 6...♝xa3! 7 bxa3 ♕d4, forking knight and rook.

15) He loses a piece: 5 ♘xd4?? e5! 6 ♝xe5 and the queen check 6...♕a5+ wins the loose bishop.

16) The queen, which White exploits with 16 ♗xc6! ♝xc6 (or 16...♕xc6 17 ♝xe7) 17 ♘e5 and the queen can't cover both bishops: 17...♕c7 18 ♝xe7 ♕xe7 19 ♘xc6, winning material.

17) Because after 7 ♗d3? ♗xd3 8 ♕xd3 e5! Black wins a piece with a pawn fork, thanks to the c3-knight being pinned: 9 dxe5 dxe5 10 ♗g3 e4 and a knight is lost. 9 b4 ♕a3 changes nothing because the knight is still pinned, now against the queen.

18) Since after 10 ♗d3?? cxd4 11 cxd4? (but otherwise White has lost a key pawn for nothing) 11...♕c3+ the only move that protects the rook is 12 ♗d2, but this also blocks the queen's protection of the d3-bishop, so 12...♕xd3 leaves Black a piece up. And after 12 ♕d2 ♕xa1 13 0-0 White has no hope of trapping the queen on a1, as there are too many light squares to cover.

19) Black has walked into a nasty double attack: 9 e5! ♗xf3 (if the knight moves, White plays 10 ♕xg4) and now 10 exf6! is the key point. White is still attacking two pieces at once, and so wins a piece.

20) There certainly is: 9 ♖xg7?? loses a piece after 9...♕f6!. If you thought 10 ♖xh7 ♖xh7 11 ♕xh7 would save White, then 11...♘f8!, followed by ...♕xf3 after the queen retreats, would leave you highly disappointed.

21) Yes, there is a great difference. 5 ♘xe5?? is a blunder because 5...d4 wins a piece since if the knight moves from c3, 6...♕a5+ will fork and win the knight on e5. 5 cxd5! is best. After 5...cxd5 6 ♘xe5 d4 White saves his knight with the vital queen check 7 ♕a4+; e.g., 7...♘c6 8 ♘xc6 bxc6 9 ♘e4 with a good extra pawn.

22) 8...c6? allows a nasty tactic that wins material: 9 ♘f6+! gxf6 10 ♕xd8+ ♔xd8 11 ♗xf6+ and this fork leaves White rook for bishop up, though Black can put up resistance. 8...♘d7! is a good move, which makes it hard for White to prove he has enough active play to make up for being a pawn down.

23) 9...♕a5+?? is a mistake because after 10 ♗d2! ♕xa2 11 ♖xb2 (11 c3, intending ♕c2, is also winning) 11...♕xb2 the deadly bishop fork 12 ♗c3 leaves White a piece up. 9...♗g7 is best. After 10 ♗xc5 d6 material is level and Black isn't much worse.

24) It doesn't look like a position where White might have an instant win, but 8...♘ge7?? weakens Black's control of the d6-square, and so invites 9 ♗xc4!. The point is that 9...dxc4 10 ♘xc4 forks the queen and the d6-square, and after 10...♕a6 11 ♘d6+ ♔d8 a further fork picks up the rook in the corner: 12 ♘xf7+ ♔c7 13 ♘xh8. White would have a big material plus even if Black could trap the knight in the corner – which he can't.

25) No, because after 12 h3? ♗xf3 13 ♕xf3 Black wins a piece with 13...e5! because White's pieces will be forked. ...exd4 and ...e4 are both threats, and 14 dxe5 ♘xe5 15 ♕f4 ♘h5 16 ♕b4 ♘xd3 17 cxd3 d4 is a decisive pawn fork.

26) True. Surprisingly, White has no way to defend his pawns on b2 and e5. The main point is 10 b3?? ♕d4!, forking bishop and rook. Otherwise, 10 ♗c1 abandons the e5-pawn, 10 0-0 ♕xb2 11 ♘d2 ♘xe5 gives Black a big advantage, while 10 ♕c1 is met with 10...♕b8 followed by ...♘xe5 and ...♗d6 with a good extra pawn (10...♖b8 11 ♘d2! ♕xb2 12 ♕xb2 ♖xb2 13 ♘b3 is less clear).

27) 7...♘h4! 8 h3 (or 8 ♕xh4 ♘xg2+ and ...♘xh4; 8 ♕f3 ♘xg2+ 9 ♔xg2 ♕xc4 exploits the loose bishop) 8...h5! (forcing White's hand; 8...♘xg2+? 9 ♔f1 h5 10 ♕e2 ♘f4 11 ♕e3! is much less clear) 9 ♕xh4 ♘xg2+ 10 ♔e2 ♘xh4 and Black has won a good pawn.

28) 8 ♕b3?! ♗d5 offers White little, while 8 ♕a4+?! is tempting, but 8...♘c6! 9 ♘xc6 ♕d7! is far from clear. The right path is 8 ♘xf7! ♔xf7, when both 9 ♕b3+ ♗d5 10 ♘g5+

and 9 ♘g5+ (since 9...♔g6 10 ♕c2+ ♔xg5 11 d4+ leads to mate) win back the piece with a huge advantage.

29) False. 10...♗e6?? walks into a pawn fork: 11 d4 exd4 12 exd4 and after the bishop retreats (e.g., 12...♗a7) the pawn advance 13 d5 wins a piece.

30) 11...♗a6! is good because one way or another White will have to allow a deadly discovery on the long diagonal: 12 ♖f2? dxe3 is a double attack on rook and bishop, while 12 ♗e2? ♗xe2 13 ♕xe2 d3 hits queen and bishop. That leaves just the appalling 12 d3? ♘xe3 and 12 ♗xd5 ♗xf1 13 ♗xc6 ♖c8, with a material advantage for Black.

31) 10 ♗xc5! ♕xc5 11 ♕d4! and there is no good move for Black. The white queen threatens to take on c5 or e5, and the obvious reply 11...♕xd4 12 cxd4 leaves Black threatened with both dxe5 and ♘xc7+.

32) 15 ♗xh6! wins a key pawn in front of Black's king. The basic point is 15...gxh6? 16 ♖xd7! ♕xd7 17 ♘f6+, winning the queen. After 15...♘cxe5 16 ♘xe5 ♘xe5 one good option is 17 ♘g5 with ♗xb7 to follow. Note that switching the move-order with 15 ♖xd7? ♕xd7 16 ♗xh6 is not so good because Black can ignore the bishop by 16...♖ed8 intending ...♕d3.

33) After 13 ♖xe6+! fxe6 14 ♘xe6 the knights coordinate tremendously, as the possible fork on c7 prevents the queen from capturing either of them: 14...♕d6 (14...♕xd5? 15 ♘xc7+; 14...♕d7 15 ♘dxc7+ ♔f7 16 ♘g5+ ♔g8 17 ♘xa8 with a material plus and an attack) 15 ♗f4! ♘e5 (15...♕xc6? 16 ♘xc7!) 16 ♕c2 and White wins the e5 knight, with his own knights still dominant.

34) No, because after 12 dxe5 dxe5 13 ♘xe5?? the retreat 13...♘c7! creates a double attack and wins a piece.

35) False! 12 ♗xh6! wins a pawn because after 12...♘xe4 13 ♘xe4 ♕h4+ 14 g3 ♕xh6 the fact that the rook is on e8 means that 15 ♕xh6 ♗xh6 16 ♘f6+ wins material. In *Chess Opening Traps for Kids*, we saw a similar example where the knight fork won a loose bishop on d7.

36) No, but it is very risky. After 9...♘xc3 White has the reply 10 ♘g5! threatening both mate with ♕xh7# and material gain with ♗xb7. Often this idea is a clear win, but Black can defend here with 10...♘e4!. Then 11 ♗xe4 ♗xe4 12 ♕xe4 ♕xg5 13 ♕xa8 ♘c6 14 ♕b7 leads to a complicated game where both players will need to be careful.

DOUBLE ATTACK

4 Trapped Pieces

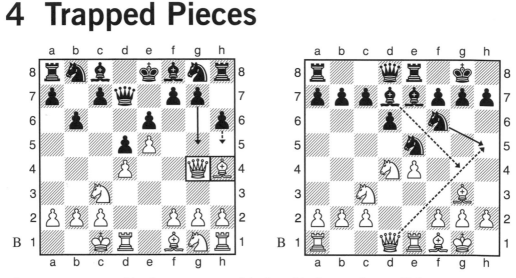

Pieces can get trapped in almost any part of the board in the opening, and it happens at all levels of chess, from beginner to grandmaster. The most dramatic is when a queen makes a raid into enemy territory to win a pawn or a piece, but finds its route back to safety suddenly blocked off. We see many examples like that in this chapter. Even a queen in the middle of the board can sometimes be trapped, despite its great mobility. There are also cases where pieces get slaughtered in their beds without ever having moved, blocked in by their own pawns.

A common way to win a bishop is seen in our first diagram above. Despite his lack of development, Black can trap the wayward white bishop with his pawns: 8...g5! 9 ♗g3 h5! (the white queen proves fatally misplaced) 10 ♕f3 (10 ♕xg5? ♗h6 pins and wins the queen, while 10 ♕h3? hopes to save the bishop by a pin on the h-file, but leaves the queen trapped after 10...g4 11 ♕h4 ♗e7) 10...h4 and the bishop is lost. So be careful when you place a bishop in front of your own pawns!

The second diagram features an important queen-trapping theme. 11...♘h5! is a good move, as it prepares to exchange the powerful bishop on g3 and frees Black's own bishop on e7. But what happens if White takes the knight? After 12 ♕xh5?? ♗g4 the white queen is trapped and lost. This pattern is quite common when a queen ventures to h5 early in the game, and we shall see several more examples. Note that spotting this clever tactic meant that Black was able to play a very useful move in a position where otherwise he would have been cramped.

- When a piece has only one way back to safety, it is in great danger of being trapped.
- A rook or bishop in front of its pawns can get caught in no man's land. A rook tends to come under attack by the enemy minor pieces, while pawns are the bishop's natural enemy.
- Don't be fooled by the queen's great mobility. Its equally great value means that the opponent can make considerable sacrifices to trap the queen and still emerge ahead on material.
- Pieces that have never moved can also be trapped, especially when they are boxed in by their own pawns.

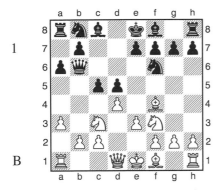

1

White has just played 6 a3. Has he overlooked the attack on his b2-pawn?

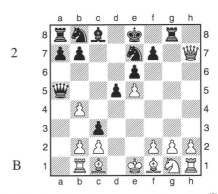

2

Can Black play a better move than 10...♛xb4 here?

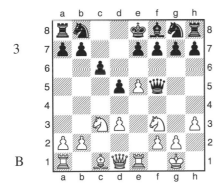

3

"Black plays 10...c6 and continues his development safely." True or false?

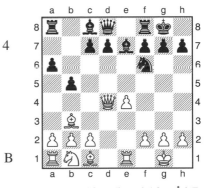

4

Choose between 10...c5 and 10...♝b7.

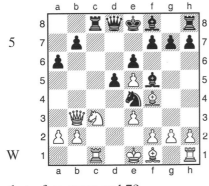

5

Is that a free pawn on b7?

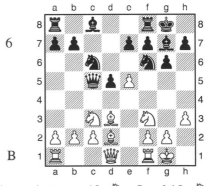

6

Choose between 10...♞xe5 and 10...♞d7.

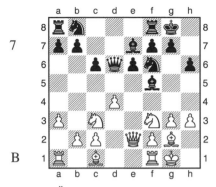

7

"After 11...♘bd7 Black will finish developing with no problems." True or false?

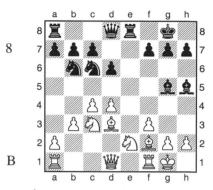

8

Is 13...♗e3 a useful way to exchange bishops and free Black's game?

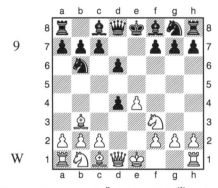

9

W

Choose between 6 ♘xd4 and 6 ♕xd4.

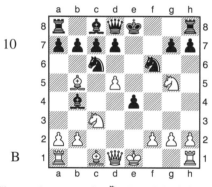

10

B

Choose between 9...♘e7 and 9...h6.

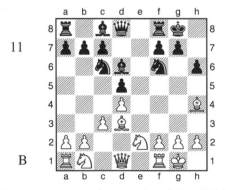

11

B

Do you see a good way to break into White's kingside?

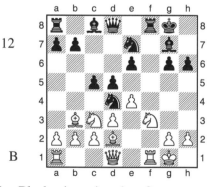

12

B

Can Black win a piece here?

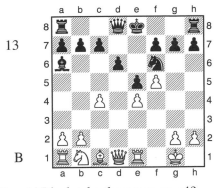

13   B

Should Black take the pawn on c4?

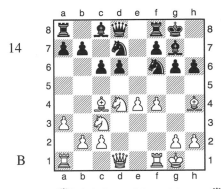

14   B

Does 11...♕b6 followed by either ...♕xb2 or ...♘xe4 win a pawn?

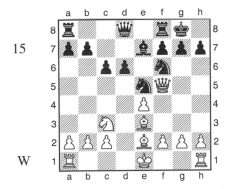

15   W

Should White play 11 f4, pushing back the black knight?

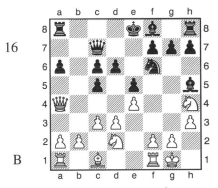

16   B

Is it a good idea to play 11...♗c2 and grab the d3-pawn?

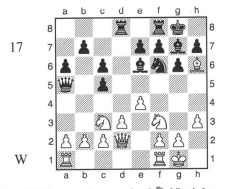

17   W

Can White use the standard ♘d5 trick to win a pawn on e7?

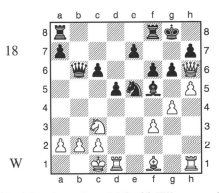

18   W

Black has just played 16...f6. Why wasn't he worried about White taking his bishop?

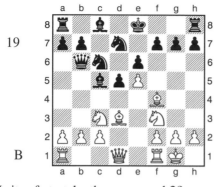

19
B

Is it safe to take the pawn on b2?

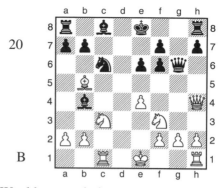

20
B

Would you grab that pawn on g2?

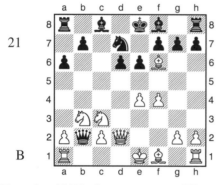

21
B

How should Black recapture on f6?

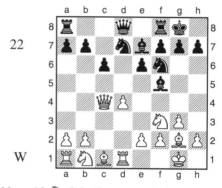

22
W

Now 10 ♘c3 is the most obvious move for White. Would you play it?

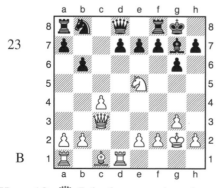

23
B

Here 12...♕c7 looks tempting, but does White's reply 13 ♕f3 put you off it?

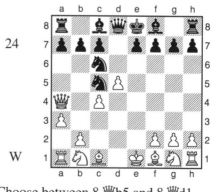

24
W

Choose between 8 ♕b5 and 8 ♕d1.

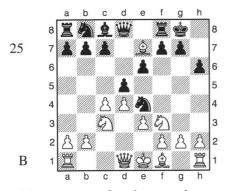

25

In this sequence of exchanges, do you play 8...♕xe7 or 8...♘xc3 here?

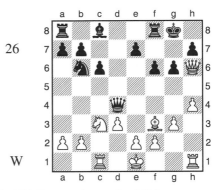

26

Is 15 h5 a good way for White to press forward with his attack?

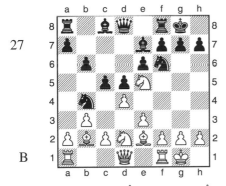

27

Choose between 10...♗a6 and 10...♗b7.

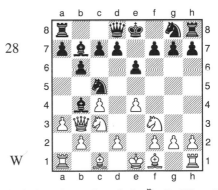

28

Black has just played 6...♘c5. Was this a mistake?

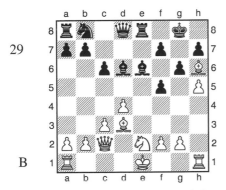

29

White has just put his bishop on h6, smelling the black king's blood. But which piece is really in danger?

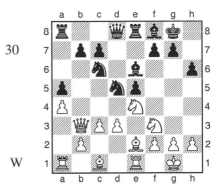

30

Black has just played his bishop to e6, offering the b7-pawn. What happens if White takes it?

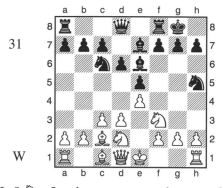

31

Is 9 ♘xe5 a clever way to grab a pawn?

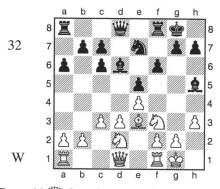

32

Does 11 ♕b3+ win a pawn?

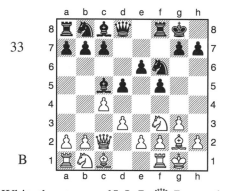

33

White threatens cxd5. Is 7...♕e7 a good way to defend the bishop?

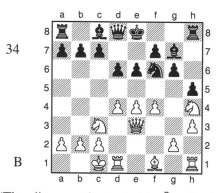

34

"The discovered attack 11...♘xe4 wins a pawn." True or false?

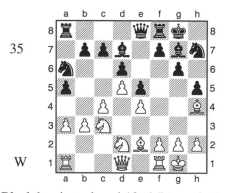

35

Black has just played 13...h5 to activate his bishop on h6. Does the move have any other ideas?

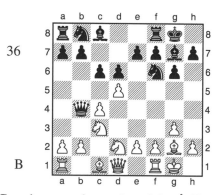

36

Grandmasters have played 9...♗d7 10 e4 a5 here. What's wrong with the immediate 9...a5?

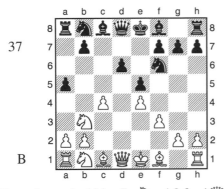

37

B

Does the typical idea 7...♘xe4 8 fxe4 ♛h4+ work here?

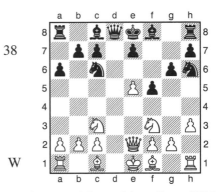

38

W

What feature of the position allows White to win a piece?

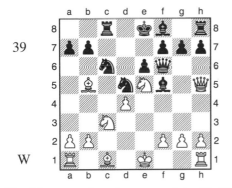

39

W

Black's queen has just moved to f6. What happened next?

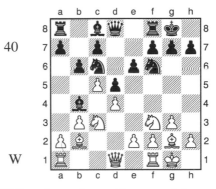

40

W

White wins a piece with a surprising move.

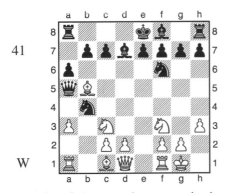

41

W

"Black is safe because the a-pawn is pinned." True or false?

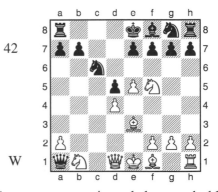

42

W

An accurate move is needed to trap the black queen.

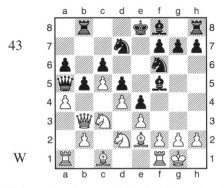

43

White wins in surprisingly dramatic fashion.

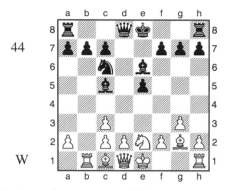

44

Is that a free pawn on b7?

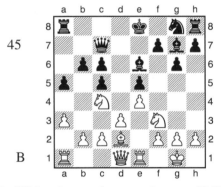

45

Is White threatening to take on e5? If so, does 11...b5 address that threat?

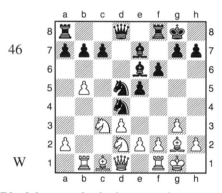

46

Black has overlooked a strong but surprising idea. What is it?

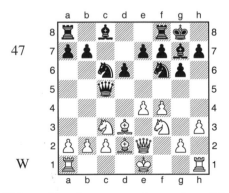

47

This position has occurred a number of times but White has only found the forced win in one game. Can you?

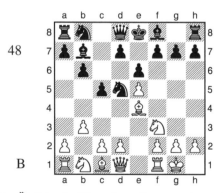

48

7...♘e3 looks like a tempting way to exploit the loose bishop on e4. Should you play it?

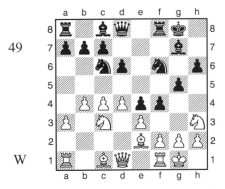

49

Black is threatening 12...f3. But after 12 exf4 what is his idea?

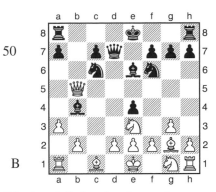

50

White has failed to develop and gone pawn-grabbing. Hunt down that queen!

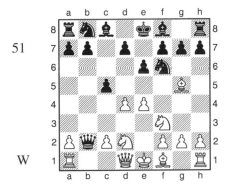

51

Black has just grabbed a pawn on b2 and his queen looks safe enough. But is it?

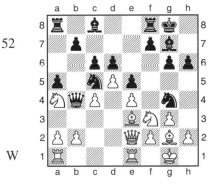

52

How do you trap the black queen?

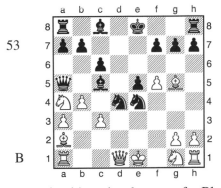

53

An amazing idea wins the game for Black.

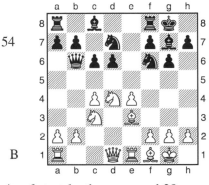

54

Is it safe to take the pawn on b2?

Solutions to Trapped Piece Exercises

1) No, because after 6...♕xb2?? 7 ♘a4 the queen is trapped.

2) Definitely, as 10...♕a2! traps the white rook on b1.

3) False. After 10...e6? 11 ♘h4 Black's queen is trapped.

4) This should not have been a difficult decision, because 10...c5! followed by 11...c4 wins a piece. This is one of many forms of the Noah's Ark Trap.

5) No, it is a very costly one! After 12 ♕xb7?? ♘c5! White's queen is trapped following 13 ♕a7 ♖a8, while 13 ♗g5 ♘xb7 and 13 ♗b5+ axb5 14 ♕xb5+ ♕d7 leave White a piece down.

6) 10...♘d7?? loses on the spot because 11 ♘a4! traps the queen. 10...♘xe5! is the right move. The point is revealed after 11 ♘xe5 d4, regaining the piece thanks to the double attack on the white knights.

7) False. 11...♘bd7?? is a terrible mistake as it cuts off the queen's retreat, and 12 ♗f4! wins on the spot. 11...♕c7 is one good option for Black, with developing moves to follow. The loss of time matters little, as White's play has been slow too.

8) No, because after 13...♗e3?? 14 ♗xe3 ♖xe3 15 ♗e4! the rook is stuck in hostile territory and will soon be lost.

9) The problem with 6 ♘xd4? is that it walks into a relative of the Noah's Ark Trap: 6...c5! 7 ♘b5 c4 traps the bishop. 6 ♕xd4 is the right recapture. After 6...c5 White can reply 7 ♕d3, when there is no danger of his bishop being trapped.

10) 9...♘e7?? allows White to win the black queen by 10 ♘e6! thanks to the pin on the d7-pawn. 9...h6! is far better, and keeps Black fully in the game; e.g., 10 dxc6 (not 10 ♘e6? dxe6 11 dxc6 ♕xd1+ 12 ♔xd1 0-0) 10...hxg5 11 cxb7 (or 11 cxd7+ ♗xd7) 11...♗xb7 12 ♗xg5 c6 13 ♗e2 d5.

11) 9...♗xh2+! has a different idea from most ...♗xh2+ sacrifices: to trap the white bishop on h4! After 10 ♔xh2 ♘g4+ 11 ♔g3 (11 ♔h3 ♘e3+ 12 ♔g3 ♕d6+ costs White his queen) 11...g5! Black will regain his bishop while keeping an attack against the hopelessly placed white king. 12 ♖h1 (or 12 ♗xg5 ♕xg5 13 f4 ♕g7 and ...♖e8) and now 12...♕d6+ 13 f4 ♖e8 is the strongest of many good options.

12) Yes, with 12...c4! 13 dxc4 (13 ♗a4 is no better due to 13...b5! 14 ♗xb5 ♘xb5 15 ♘xb5 ♕b6+) 13...dxc4 14 ♗xc4 ♘xf3+ 15 ♖xf3 ♕d4+ and Black picks off the loose bishop.

13) No, since after 12...♗xc4? 13 ♕a4+ b5 14 ♕c2! the bishop has no escape and will be won by playing b3. Black will have three pawns for the bishop, but in a middlegame this is not enough.

14) No, because 11...♕b6 does not actually threaten to take on b2. After 12 ♗f2! the black queen is misplaced and will soon have to move again, since 12...♕xb2?? 13 ♘a4 walks into a standard trap.

15) No, 11 f4?? is a terrible error, allowing the queen to be trapped by 11...♘fg4! intending ...g6. Then 12 ♗xg4 g6 13 fxe5 gxf5 14 ♗xf5 gives White just two pieces for the queen.

16) No, 11...♗e2? 12 ♖e1 ♗xd3 is a bad idea since 13 c4 traps the bishop. He can salvage it by playing 13...d5 but this rips his position apart and exposes his king.

17) No, because after 12 ♘d5?! ♕xd2 13 ♘xe7+?? ♔h8 14 ♗xd2 ♖fe8 the knight is trapped.

48

18) 17 gxf5?? loses because 17...g5! walls in the white queen, and ...♘f7 will win it.

19) 9...♕xb2?? is a blunder even though it looks like the queen has enough escape squares, such as a3 and b4. However, 10 ♘b5! covers a3 while gaining time by threatening ♘c7+. After 10...♖b8 11 ♗d2 the queen has no way out and will be lost. After 11...d4 (preventing 12 ♗c3, which would be the answer to 11...a6 and 11...♘dxe5) 12 ♕e2 the plan is ♖fb1, and it is an unstoppable juggernaut.

20) I hope you answered 'no', because after 13...♕xg2?? 14 ♖g1 (14 ♔e2 also wins) 14...♕xf3 15 ♖g3 the queen is trapped.

21) 10...♘xf6?? is a blunder because 11 a4! (or 11 a3!) intending ♖a2 traps the black queen. 10...gxf6! is essential. The difference is that now after 11 a3? Black can play 11...♘c5!, not just rescuing his queen but also shattering White's queenside. So White should choose 11 ♗e2, when he is a pawn down, but has a development advantage.

22) Even obvious moves can be terrible mistakes. After 10 ♘c3?? ♗c2! White loses material because both ...♗xd1 and ...♘b6, trapping the queen, are threatened.

23) It shouldn't! 12...♕c7! wins because after 13 ♕f3 ♗xe5 14 ♕xa8 ♘c6 the white queen is trapped.

24) With 8 ♕b5?? White hopes to win a piece but will lose his queen: 8...e5! (threatening ...a6; 8...e6! is just as good) 9 dxc6 b6! (the queen has no squares and ...a6 is coming next) 10 ♔c2 (10 ♕b4 ♘d3+) 10...a5! (clearer than 10...a6 11 ♕b4) 11 b4 ♗a6 and it's game over. 8 ♕d1! is best, as Black's knights will be driven to bad squares while White has fast development and lots of space; e.g., 8...♘e5 9 b4 ♘cd7 10 f4 ♘g6 11 ♘f3.

25) Not 8...♘xc3?? 9 ♗xd8! ♘xd1 10 ♗e7 ♖e8 (10...♘xb2 11 ♗xf8 leaves Black knight for rook down) 11 ♗a3, when we see the problem: the knight is trapped. 8...♕xe7 is necessary, and after 9 cxd5 Black should insert 9...♘xc3 before recapturing on d5.

26) No, 15 h5? is bad because 15...g5! walls in the white queen. It will be a while before Black can actually attack and win the queen, but there is no way for it to escape. As a sample line to show that White can't smash through, 16 ♗e4 ♖f7 17 ♗xh7+ ♖xh7 18 ♕g6+ ♖g7 19 ♕e8+ ♔h7 20 h6 ♗h3! neatly quashes any threats, while 16 e3 ♕b4 17 ♗e4 ♖f7 18 ♖c2 looks most resilient, but White is struggling to stay in the game.

27) With 10...♗a6?? Black is looking to exchange off his 'bad' bishop. It is not so clear that it is a bad piece, but tactical considerations are far more important in any case. 11 c3! wins a piece because 11...♗xe2 12 ♕xe2 covers the a6-square and 12...♘c2 13 ♖ac1 gives the knight no way out. 10...♗b7 is a standard developing move, giving Black a solid game.

28) No, it was a good move. 7 ♕xb4?? a5 8 ♕b5 c6 leaves the queen trapped, so White has nothing better than 7 ♕c2 ♗xc3 8 ♕xc3, when 8...♘xe4 9 ♕xg7 ♕f6 and 8...f6 9 d3 e5 both give Black a good position.

29) The bishop itself, as 12...g5! walls it in, trapping it. ...♕f6 is coming next. Then 13 ♗xf5 ♕f6 14 ♗xh7+ ♔h8 gives White three pawns for his piece, but his own king comes under immediate attack after 15 ♗g6 ♗c4 or 15 ♗xg5 ♕xg5. Also 13 f4 ♗xf4 doesn't help White since 14 ♘xf4? ♗b3+ costs him his queen. And after 13 ♕d2 f4 14 g3 ♗g4 (14...♕f6? 15 gxf4 ♕xh6 16 fxg5 is not so clear) 15 gxf4 (15 0-0-0 ♗xe2 16 ♗xe2 ♕f6) 15...♗xf4 White suffers a fatal material loss.

30) He loses his queen: 13 ♕xb7?? ♘b6! (13...♕d7, intending ...♖eb8, is also good: 14 ♕b5 ♖eb8 15 ♘c5 ♕e8 16 ♕c4 ♘e3 17 ♕e4 ♘c2) 14 ♕xc6 ♗d5 15 ♕xe8 (White must give up his queen; after 15 ♕b5 c6 it is lost for even less material) 15...♕xe8 and White doesn't have enough for the queen as his pieces are poorly placed.

31) No, it isn't. 9 ♘xe5?? ♘xe5 10 ♕xh5 (10 d4 ♘g4 11 h3 ♘g3!? gives Black a devastating counterattack) is White's idea, but the problem is that his queen is trapped by 10...♗g4!, a pattern we see elsewhere in the book.

32) No, 11 ♕b3+?! doesn't win a pawn. Black replies 11...♗f7!, when 12 ♕xb7?? ♕d7 intends ...♖fb8, trapping the white queen. 13 ♗a7 doesn't help because of 13...c5 with ...♘c6 to follow.

33) No, because the bishop is trapped after 7...♕e7? 8 d4. Then 8...♗b6 (8...♗d6 9 c5) 9 c5 ♗a5 is the trickiest line, but 10 ♕a4! ♘c6 (10...b6 11 b4) 11 ♘e5 wins a piece.

34) False, because after 11...♘xe4?? 12 ♘xe4 ♕xh4 13 ♘g5 the queen is trapped and g3 will win it. Always check the position after the tactic to make sure there is nothing unpleasant happening.

35) Yes, he is threatening to trap the white bishop! Thus 14 ♖b1?? is a terrible mistake because after 14...g5! 15 ♗g3 h4 White is losing his bishop. 14 ♔h1?? and 14 ♕c2?? are other blunders that have been made by good players. 14 f3 is the standard move, giving the bishop an escape route.

36) The problem with 9...a5?? is that 10 ♘a4! traps the queen: 10...cxd5 (or 10...b5 11 a3! ♕xa4 12 b3) 11 a3 and with no bishop on d7, the queen is trapped. Instead after 9...♗d7 10 e4 a5, 11 ♘a4? would be a mistake because of 11...cxd5 12 a3? ♕xa4.

37) Yes, it does, but for an unusual reason. After 7...♘xe4! 8 fxe4 ♕h4+, 9 g3? ♕xe4+ picks off the h1-rook, and 9 ♔e2? ♗g4+ skewers the queen, so White has to play 9 ♔d2, when 9...a4 traps the knight on b3. While Black doesn't actually win material, he has damaged White's structure and exposed his king.

38) The black queen has no escape if attacked along the d-file, so White just needs to open a path to get a rook there without losing any time. 10 ♗xh6! fits the bill, and after 10...♗xh6 11 ♖d1 ♗d7 12 e6 the black bishop is lost.

39) The queen is trapped: 11 ♗g5! ♗g6 (11...g6 12 ♗xf6 gxh5 13 ♗xh8 costs Black a rook) 12 ♕h4! ♕f5 13 ♗d3 and there is no way out.

40) 11 ♘b1! is a very strong retreat, preventing Black from exchanging on c3 and so allowing the white pawns to trap the bishop by playing a3 and b4. 11...bxc5 doesn't help because White inserts 12 a3 ♗a5 before playing 13 dxc5 and b4.

41) False, because after 10 axb4! (10 ♗xd7+ ♘xd7 11 axb4! is just as good) 10...♕xa1 11 ♗xd7+ ♘xd7 12 ♘d4! followed by ♘b3, White traps the queen on a1.

42) 10 ♕b3! (10 ♕c2? doesn't work because of 10...e6 11 ♗b5 ♗b4+ 12 ♔e2 ♖c8) 10...e6 (or 10...0-0-0 11 ♗b5! intending 0-0 and trapping the queen) 11 ♕xb7 (the key difference between putting the queen on c2 or b3) gives White a decisive attack: 11...♗b4+ 12 ♔e2 ♕xa2+ (12...♕xb1 13 ♕xc6+ and ♕xa8+) 13 ♔f3 leaves Black defenceless, or 11...♖b8 12 ♘d6+ (12 ♕xc6+ ♔d8 13 ♗d3 ♖xb1+ 14 ♗xb1 ♕xb1+ 15 ♔e2 also wins) 12...♔d8 13 ♘xf7+ ♔e8 14 ♕xc6+ ♔xf7 15 ♕c7+ and ♕xb8.

43) 12 axb5! is a deadly a-file discovery. 12...♕xa1 (otherwise White wins pawns for nothing) 13 bxc6! ♗xc5 (the key point is that 13...♖xb3 14 ♘xb3 traps the queen, so White emerges material up) 14 cxd7+ ♔xd7 15 dxc5 leaves White well ahead on material because the queen trap still works if Black takes on b3.

44) No, 9 ♖xb7?? is a blunder due to a hidden mousetrap idea: 9...♗d5! (the immediate 9...♗b6?? is no good because of the loose knight on c6) 10 0-0 (10 ♗xd5 ♕xd5 comes to the same thing as after White saves his h1-rook, 11...♗b6 will trap the other rook) 10...♗xg2 11 ♔xg2 ♕d5+ 12 ♔g1 ♗b6 and the white rook is lost: Black can even attack it by castling!

45) First question: yes, 12 ♘cxe5 (not 12 ♘fxe5? b5) is a threat because of the long-diagonal skewer after 12...♗xe5 13 ♘xe5 ♕xe5 14 ♗c3. Second question: yes again, since after 11...b5 White can't play 12 ♘cxe5?? because 12...f6 traps the knight now that the c4-square is covered.

46) After 13 ♗xd5! ♗xd5 14 e3 Black loses a piece: 14...♘e6 15 e4 or 14...♘f5 15 ♘xd5 ♕xd5 16 e4.

47) 12 ♘a4! ♘d4 (the queen has no safe squares; 12...♕h5 13 0-0-0 followed by g4 also costs Black material) 13 ♘xd4! ♕xd4 14 c4! cuts the queen off from b4 and a4. White threatens both ♗c3 and ♗e3, so even with a free move Black has no good way to save his queen.

48) No, 7...♘e3? is bad because White gives up his queen, getting much more than enough in return: 8 ♗xb7! ♘xd1 9 ♗xa8 and the knight is trapped. After 9...g5 10 ♖xd1 g4 11 ♘e1 ♗g7 12 c3 ♗xe5 13 d4 the game continues, but Black is worse.

49) 12 exf4 g4 traps the knight – a standard theme in this pawn-structure, which arises in several openings.

50) 11...♖b8 is strong. After 12 ♕g5 Black has several good options, including 12...♗f8! followed by ...h6, running the queen out of squares (e.g., 13 ♘c2 h6 14 ♕e3 ♖b3 15 d3 exd3 16 exd3 ♘g4) and 12...♗e7! 13 ♕xg7 ♖g8 14 ♕h6 ♖g6 15 ♕h4 ♖b5, when the queen will not survive long. The other key point is 12 ♕a4 ♗b3! 13 ♕xb3 ♗xd2+ 14 ♗xd2 ♖xb3.

51) No, because White covers the queen's escape squares in record time: 6 ♘c4! ♕b4+ (6...♕b5 7 ♘d6+ is a discovered attack) 7 c3! (both covering the a4-square and dragging the queen to a worse square; this is like the 'b4 Shocker' theme in *Chess Opening Traps for Kids*) 7...♕xc3+ 8 ♗d2 and the queen is trapped. Bishop retreats are easily overlooked.

52) After 16 ♗xc5! dxc5 17 ♕d1! the threat is a3, and taking on c4 doesn't help Black because ♗f1 then traps the queen in any case: 17...cxd5 (or 17...b5 18 a3 ♕xa4 19 b3) 18 a3 ♕xc4 19 ♗f1. The difficulty here was that when trapping a queen, we want to keep every square covered, so realizing that we can abandon the c4-pawn is a little tricky.

53) 13...♕xa4!! wins material. Why? Because 14 ♕xa4 ♘xc3 15 ♕a5 b6 traps the white queen in a most surprising fashion!

54) No. The queen gets trapped after 11...♕xb2?? 12 ♘a4 ♕a3 (12...♕b4 13 ♗d2 is the same) 13 ♗c1! ♕b4 14 ♗d2 ♕a3 and the finishing touch comes from the rook: 15 ♖e3.

5 General Tactics

While double attack is the most common chess tactic, it is far from the only one. In this large chapter we shall see skewers, pins, discovered attacks, decoys and deflections in action. Actually, we have seen all of these in previous chapters, but here they take centre stage. We shall also see positions where many tactics are used together to devastating effect.

In our first diagram above, Black has two ways to win, each based on a different tactical theme to exploit the same weakness in White's position. 8...♗xc3+! 9 bxc3 ♘xd5! wins a pawn, thanks to two *pins*. 10 f3 is neatly met by 10...♘b6. The other way is 8...♘xd5!? 9 ♕xb4 (9 cxd5? ♗xc3+ wins the queen using a *discovered attack*) 9...♕xe2+ (9...♘dxb4 10 ♘xe4 ♘c2+ 11 ♔d2 ♘xa1 12 ♔c3 is a little less clear) 10 ♗xe2 ♘dxb4 with a safe extra pawn.

In the second diagram, 9...♕xb2? doesn't get the queen trapped, but allows White a lot of activity for a pawn after 10 ♖b1 ♕a3 11 ♘cb5. There is something much better: 9...♘xe4! wins a far more important pawn and basically destroys White's position. Look out for this type of blow in the centre when a lot of force is trained upon a central piece. After 10 fxe4 (or 10 ♘xe4 ♗xd4 11 ♗xd4 ♕xd4; 10 ♘xc6 has many good answers, including 10...♕xc6!, attacking the bishop on c4) 10...♗xd4! 11 ♗xd4 ♕xd4! Black is simply a pawn up with the better position.

- In a *decoy*, we lure a piece to a square where something bad will happen to it. We might drag a queen to a square where we can fork it, or a king to a square where it can be mated or double checked. A *deflection* drags a piece away from a square or line, and we then take advantage of the fact that it isn't there any more. For both decoys and deflections, thinking in terms of 'What if...' can be very helpful.

- In the opening, especially with few pieces deployed, pins are mighty powerful. We shall see examples where the defences collapse completely under the weight of several pins.

- Be on the lookout for *pin-breaking* themes. Typically this is where a piece is pinned against a queen, but suddenly moves to create a very strong threat.

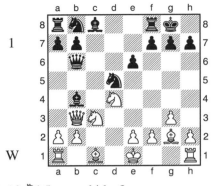

1

Is 10 ♘b5 a good idea?

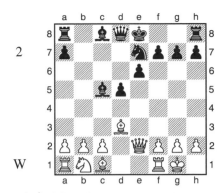

2

Is 10 ♗xh7 a clever way to win a pawn or just wishful thinking?

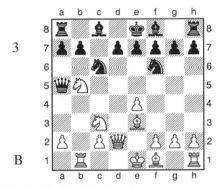

3

Black is behind in development so must be very careful. What's wrong with 9...a6 here?

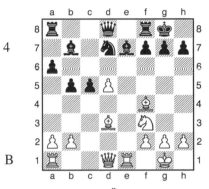

4

Black now played 15...♘f6, attacking White's d-pawn. Was this a good idea?

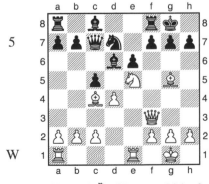

5

Is the sacrifice 13 ♘xf7 a good idea?

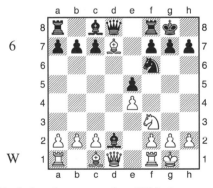

6

Black has been copying White's moves so far. Show why this was a really bad idea!

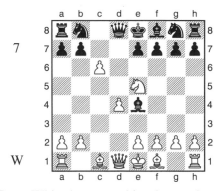

7

Does White have anything better than getting two pawns for a piece?

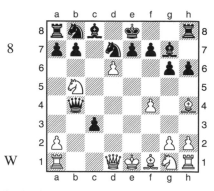

8

What's the best way to parry Black's threat of ...c2+?

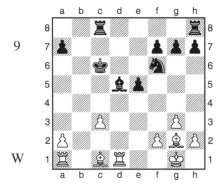

9

White can win material thanks to a pin.

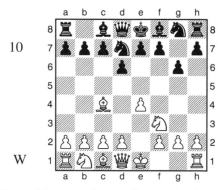

10

Does this remind you of a standard opening trap? What do you play?

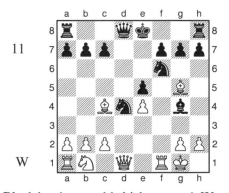

11

Black has just put his bishop on g4. Was this wise?

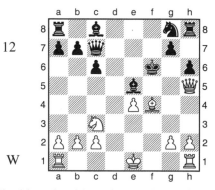

12

The king should not be used to defend central squares in the opening! Show why.

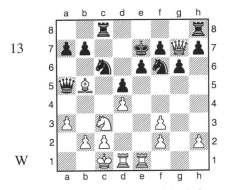

13

How would you shatter Black's defences?

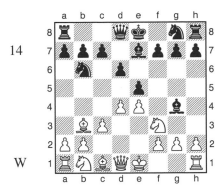

14

Black has just pinned White's knight with 6...♗g4. Was this a good idea?

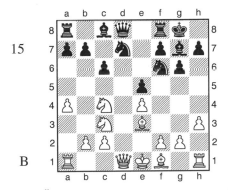

15

Is 10...♘e8 a good way to keep the white knight out of d6?

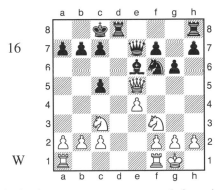

16

A single move exposes many defects in the black position.

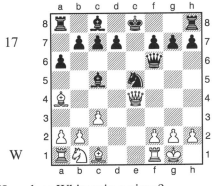

17

How does White win a piece?

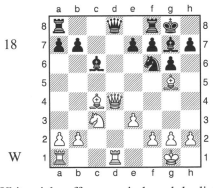

18

White picks off a pawn in broad daylight.

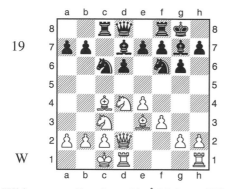

19

White normally plays 11 ♗b3 here. Why is 11 ♔b1?? a terribly careless mistake?

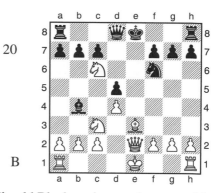

20

Should Black exchange pieces on c3 before recapturing on c6?

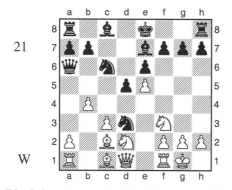

21

Black has just sunk his knight into d3, but White has a clever way to win a piece.

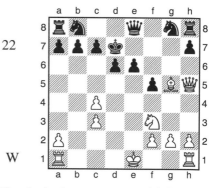

22

What is the best way to avoid the exchange of queens?

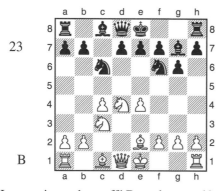

23

Loose pieces drop off! But where and how?

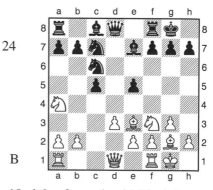

24

Is 10...b6 safe or should Black be worried about 11 ♘xe5 in reply?

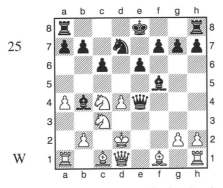

25

The black queen seems safe thanks the pin by the b4-bishop. But what if...?

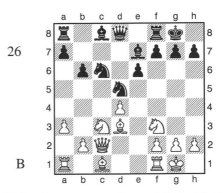

26

White threatens to take on h7. Is 11...h6 a good defence?

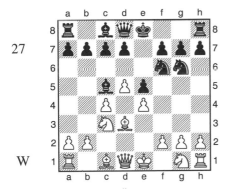

27

White has played 7 ♘gc2 in many games. How should Black answer?

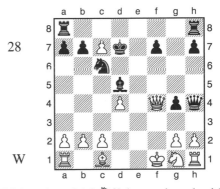

28

White played 14 ♘f3 but resigned without waiting for the reply. Why?

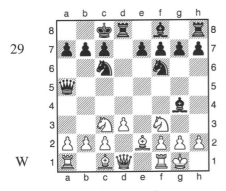

29

Do you see a weakness and a way to attack it?

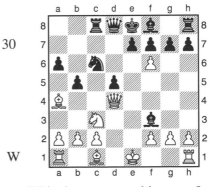

30

Does White have to move his queen?

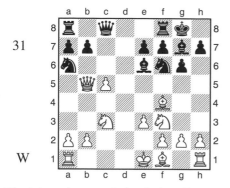

31

Black is trying to win back the c5-pawn, but has missed an important point.

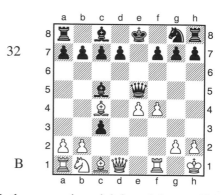

32

Is the promotion trick 9...cxb2 a good idea?

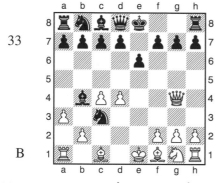

33

Choose between 6...♗a5 and 6...♗e7.

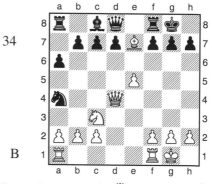

34

Choose between 12...♕xe7 and 12...♘xc3.

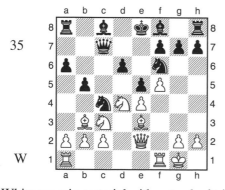

35

White can win material with a standard trick.

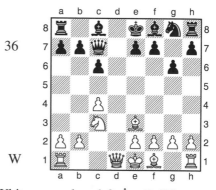

36

White now played 8 ♗xa7. What was his idea, and why doesn't it work?

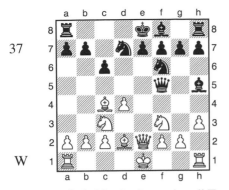

37

"The pawn fork 10 g4 wins a piece." True or false?

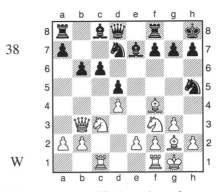

38

White uses a modified version of a standard theme.

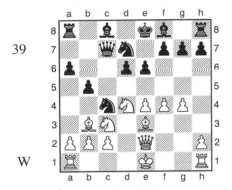

39

Does the ♘xb5 trick (which we saw in Exercise 35) work here?

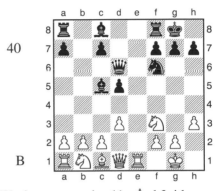

40

We have seen the 11...♗xh3 idea several times already. Is it good here?

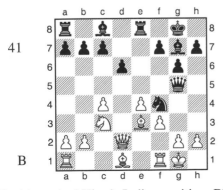

41

In this typical King's Indian position, Black has a brilliant winning move.

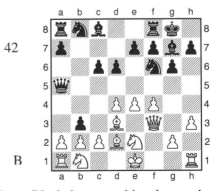

42

Does Black have anything better than retreating his queen, and losing the b3-pawn?

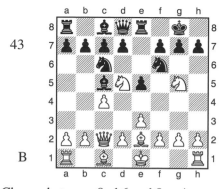

43

Choose between 8...h6 and 8...e4.

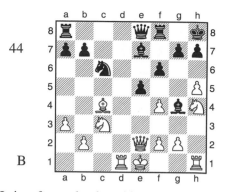

44

Is it safe to take the white queen on e2?

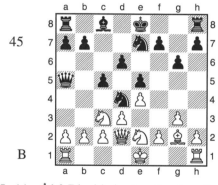

45

Is 11...♗h3 Black's best option here?

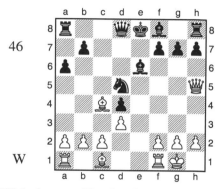

46

White has sacrificed a piece. What is his silent but deadly follow-up?

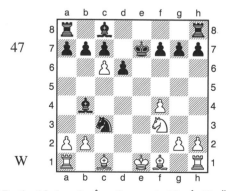

47

Both 12 bxc3 ♗xc3+ and 12 ♗d2 ♘d5 leave White material down. Does he have anything better?

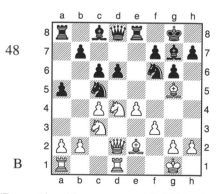

48

"By putting his queen on d2, White has secured the d4-knight and g5-bishop." True or false?

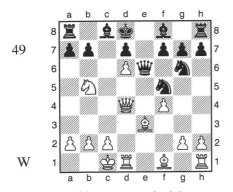

49

How does White set up a decisive see-saw?

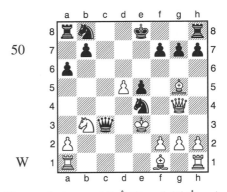

50

Choose between 15 ♗d3 and 15 ♔xe4.

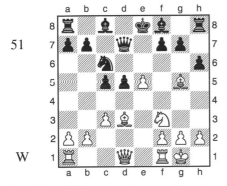

51

How does White smash open lines towards the black king?

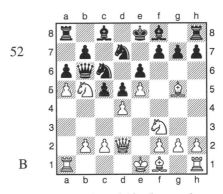

52

White has just played 10 a5, seeming to win material. What is Black's best reply?

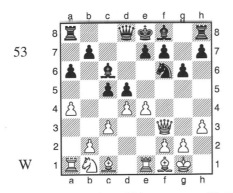

53

Black has just played his pawn to d5. This runs into problems because of a pin. How and where?

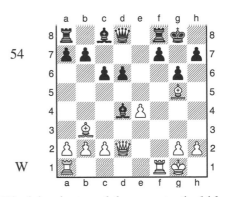

54

Black has just used the same tactical idea as in Exercise 48. Play continued 14 ♕xd4 ♕xg5. What had both players missed?

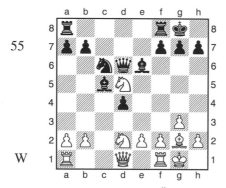

55

White normally plays 14 ♘f4 here. But doesn't 14 ♘e4 win material?

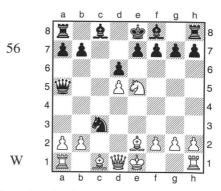

56

Does White have anything better than the obvious 10 bxc3 here?

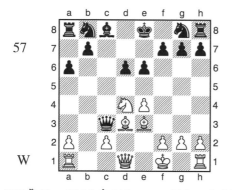

57

"10 ♘f5 exf5 11 ♗d4 is a good idea, forking c3 and g7." True or false?

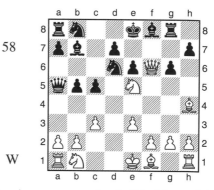

58

A crisp move overloads Black's position to breaking point.

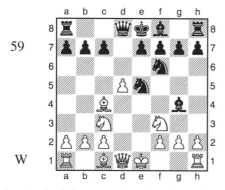

59

A standard but spectacular idea wins the game for White.

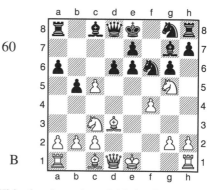

60

White has just played 10 dxc5. Why does he want to open the d-file?

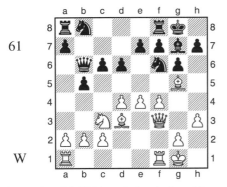

61

How should White defend the d4-pawn? Choose between 11 ♘e2 and 11 ♕f2.

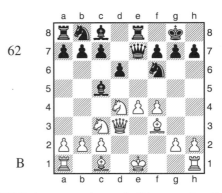

62

White's e-pawn is weak. Do you play 9...d5 or 9...♘xe4 here?

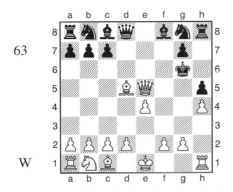

63

White wins with a deflection that is simple yet hard to spot.

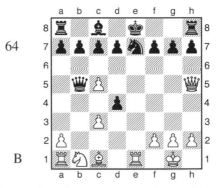

64

Remember the *en passant* rules, and choose between 12...d5 and 12...d6.

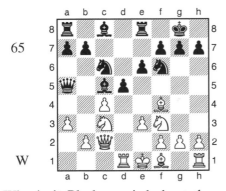

65

Why isn't Black worried about the pawn fork 11 b4 here?

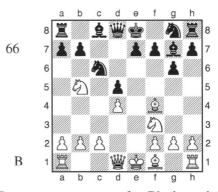

66

Do you see any way for Black to defend against White's threat of 8 ♘c7+ here?

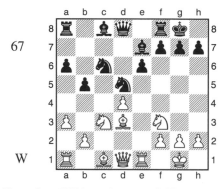

67

How does White win material?

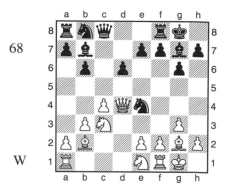

68

Does Black really get the better of the dog-fight on the long diagonals?

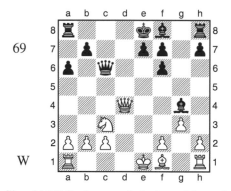

69

Should White be worried about his rook on h1?

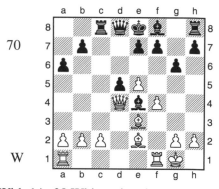

70

With 14 c3? White missed a great opportunity. What was it?

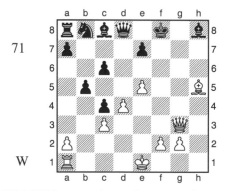

71

With White two pieces down, precise play is needed in this king-hunt.

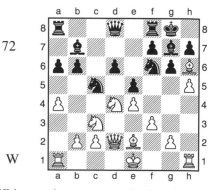

72

White carries out a standard and deadly attack.

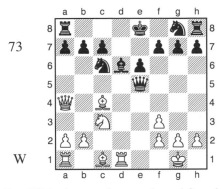

73

Can White ignore the attack on h2 and pursue his own plans?

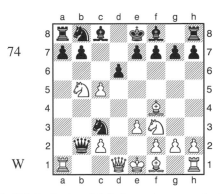

74

Is White in trouble? A neat move clarifies matters.

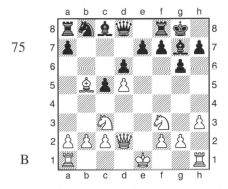

75

One good move is all it takes to bring White's position to its knees.

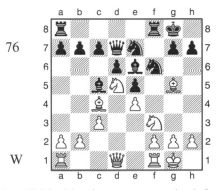

76

Are all Black's pieces as securely defended as they look?

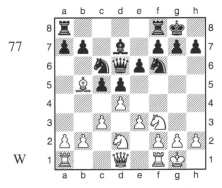

77

Is Black threatening anything? Choose between 10 ♖e1 and 10 a4.

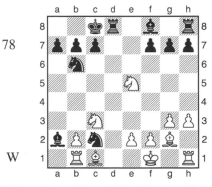

78

White resigned here. Was that justified?

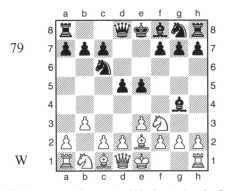

79

White can win material, but check for a sting in the tail!

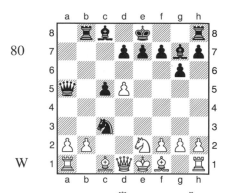

80

Choose between 11 ♕d2 and 11 ♘xc3.

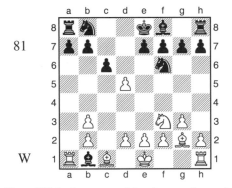

81

Does White have anything better than taking the black bishop?

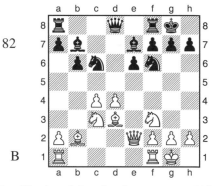

82

Can Black safely take the pawn on d4?

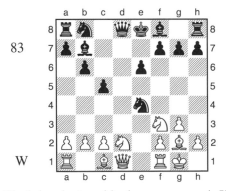

83

Black has just grabbed a pawn on e4. How do you punish him?

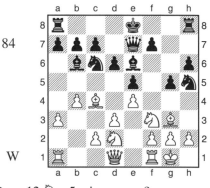

84

Does 12 ♘xe5 win a pawn?

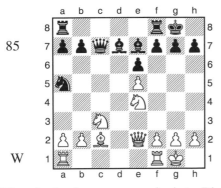

85

What is the best way to rip into Black's kingside?

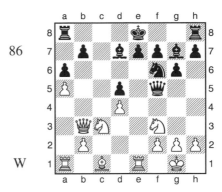

86

White exploits Black's slow development with a dramatic piece of tactics.

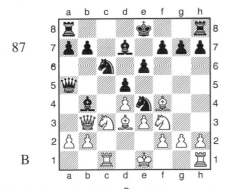

87

Black has tried 11...♘xd4 in a number of games. Do you see the idea? Does it work?

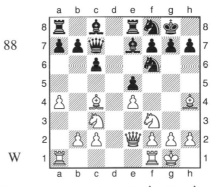

88

We have seen the idea 12 ♗xf7+ ♚xf7 13 ♕c4+ before. Is it good here?

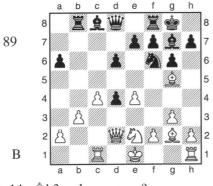

89

Is 14...♗h3 a clever move?

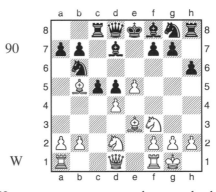

90

Use pawn power to smash open the black king's defences!

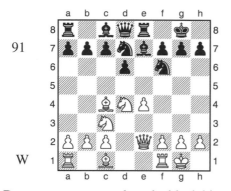

91

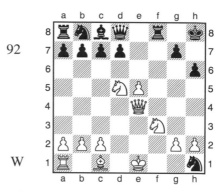

92

Do you see a way to drag the black king out into the open? Do you play it?

White is better developed and Black's king is poorly defended. Look for a forced win.

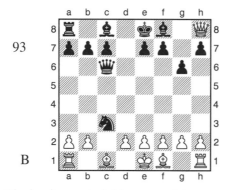

93

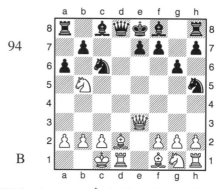

94

Black wins material in a surprising way.

White threatens ♗c3. How do you deal with this?

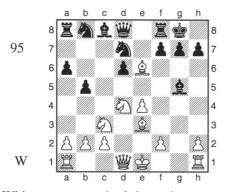

95

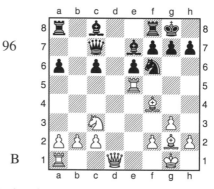

96

White uses a standard theme in an unusual setting.

Rather than move his own queen, Black plays 13...♖d8. What happens next?

Solutions to General Tactics Exercises

1) Certainly not, because 10 ♘b5?? loses a piece due to the pin after 10...♕xb5.

2) 10 ♗xh7?? is a fatal error. The idea 'works' in that 10...♖xh7? 11 ♕b5+ followed by 12 ♕xc5 does win a pawn for White, though even then Black has strong play on the h-file. But Black does not have to take the bishop right away. After 10...♗d6! (or 10...♕c7!) White has only succeeded in opening the h-file to give Black a mating attack against h2. One game ended 11 ♗d3 (or 11 ♕h5 g6 12 ♕h4 ♘f5) 11...♗xh2+ 12 ♔h1 ♕c7 13 ♕f3 ♗g1+! 0-1.

3) 9...a6? loses to 10 ♗b6! because after 10...♕xb6 the discovered attack 11 ♘d6+ wins the black queen.

4) No, 15...♘f6?? loses because 16 d6! traps and wins the bishop. The point is that 16...♗xd6 17 ♗xd6 ♕xd6 18 ♗xh7+! is a deadly d-file discovery, winning the queen.

5) It looks like a standard pattern: a knight sacrifice on f7 followed by crashing through on e6. However, 13 ♘xf7?? loses because of 13...♘b6!, covering e6 and knocking out the back-up for the knight's raid. Don't assume your sacrifices will be instantly accepted! Instead 13...♖xf7? allows White interesting play after 14 ♗xe6 or 14 ♖xe6.

6) 8 ♗xc8! ♖xc1 and now 9 ♕xd8! clearly breaks the symmetry. After 9...♖xd8 10 ♗xb7 ♖ab8 (10...♗xb2?? 11 ♖ab1 ♖ab8 12 ♖xb2 leaves White a piece ahead) 11 ♖fxc1 ♖xb7 12 b3 White is a good pawn up.

7) 7 ♕b3! is a double attack on b7 and f7. Black has no reply: 7...♕d5 (7...♗d5 and 7...e6 are both met by 8 cxb7) 8 ♕xb7 (not 8 cxb7?? ♕xb3) 8...f6 (8...♕xc6 9 ♘xc6 ♗xc6 10 ♕c8#) 9 ♕xa8 fxe5 10 ♕xb8+ ♔f7 11 c7 and White wins easily. The order White plays his moves matters: 7 cxb7?! ♗xb7 8 ♕b3 also targets b7 and f7, but here Black can defend with 8...♕d5.

8) White can ignore it and press ahead with his own far-advanced pawn: 12 ♘c7+ ♔f8 (12...♔d8 13 ♗xe7#) 13 dxe7+ ♔g8 14 e8♕+ ♔h7 and now with a second queen, White easily deals with Black's threat; e.g., 15 ♕e7 ♕a5 16 ♕d5, etc.

9) 17 ♖xd5! ♘xd5 18 c4 and White wins two pieces for a rook. A diagonal pin doesn't immobilize a *bishop*, but renders a *knight* helpless, and this type of rook sacrifice is a standard way to take advantage of this fact.

10) In the familiar version White's pawn is already on d4, but 4 ♗xf7+! works here anyway. 4...♔xf7 5 ♘g5+ and now 5...♔f6 is mated by 6 ♕f3+ ♔xg5 7 d4+ ♔h4 8 ♕h3#, while after 5...♔e8 6 ♘e6 or 5...♔g7 6 ♘e6+ Black loses his queen.

11) No, because it walks into a tactic based on a pin: 10 ♗xf7+!, the point being that 10...♔xf7?! 11 ♕xg4 regains the piece and leaves the black king very weak. 10...♔d7 11 ♕e1 is Black's best chance, but his king remains a problem. Instead, 10 ♕xg4?! makes use of a different pin, but after 10...♘xg4 11 ♗xf7+ ♔d7 12 ♗xd8 ♖axd8 Black is better because his knights are strong and with queens off the board his king is safe.

12) 13 ♗xe5+! ♕xe5 14 0-0+ and the queen is lost since 14...♔e6 gives White a choice of wins: the simple 15 ♕c8+ ♘e7 16 ♕xh8 or 15 ♕f7+ ♔d6 16 ♖ad1+ ♔c5 17 ♕f2+, with mate soon to follow.

13) 16 ♖xe6+! uses the pin along the seventh rank to make the black king walk the plank. 16...♔xe6 17 ♖e1+ ♔d6 (no better is 17...♔d7 18 ♕xf7+) 18 ♕xf6+ ♔c7 19 ♕f4+! ♔b6 20

♕d6 (threatening ♖e7 followed by ♕c5#) and after 20...a6 21 ♕c5+ ♔c7 22 ♖e7+ ♔b8 23 ♖xb7+ ♔xb7 24 ♗xc6+ the queen is lost.

14) No, because 7 dxe5! gives Black a big problem. 7...♗xf3 8 ♕xf3 attacks f7 so Black has no time to take on e5, while 7...dxe5 walks into the standard pin-breaking knight-fork idea: 8 ♗xf7+! (8 ♕xd8+ ♖xd8 9 ♘xe5 also leaves White a pawn up) 8...♔xf7 9 ♘xe5+, so Black remains a pawn down. Instead 7 ♗xf7+?? ♔xf7 8 dxe5 is a bad move-order because Black doesn't have to recapture on e5.

15) No, because 10...♘e8? leaves the d7-knight pinned and so allows 11 ♗c5!, winning rook for bishop.

16) With 12 ♘d5!, the knight forks the queen and knight. Black's bishop and knight are both pinned, and the d8-rook is overloaded. 12...♘xd5 (12...♗xd5? 13 ♕xe7) 13 exd5 and the bishop is lost because 13...♖xd5 allows 14 ♕xh8+.

17) With the pin on the e-file. After 11 ♗f4! Black can't play 11...d6 because this pawn is also pinned, while 11...♗d6 is answered with 12 ♖e1 followed by ♗xe5. Note that White must avoid 11 ♖e1?? ♗xf2+.

18) 13 ♗xf7+! wins a pawn because 13...♔xf7? allows 14 ♕c4+, discovering an attack on the black queen, while 13...♖xf7? abandons the rook's protection of the queen, so 14 ♕xd8+ follows.

19) 11 ♔b1?? loses a piece because 11...♘xd4! discovers an attack onto the c4-bishop, and after 12 ♕xd4 ♘g4! the queen is overloaded by the need to defend both bishops, so White loses one of them.

20) Firstly, there is no strong reason for Black to avoid the immediate 10...bxc6 as his bishop is a good piece, but far more importantly 10...♗xc3+?? is a failed in-between move (or *intermezzo*) because White replies 11 ♗d2+! and takes the black queen next move.

21) The pawn fork 12 b5! decoys the black queen to an undefended square, so after 12...♕xb5 13 ♕e2! the black knight is pinned and lost.

22) Winning the queen and forcing mate! 12 ♘e5+! dxe5 13 0-0-0+ forces the king to abandon its queen: 13...♔c6 14 ♕xe8+ ♔b6 15 ♕b5#. This was from a game of the author's played at one end of the famous Penny Lane in Liverpool.

23) 7...♘xe4! captures a pawn while discovering an attack on the d4-knight. Black wins a pawn after 8 ♘xe4 ♘xd4 or 8 ♘xc6 ♗xc3+ (8...♘xc3 is also good) 9 bxc3 dxc6!.

24) 10...b6! is a good move. It is a common blindspot, but 11 ♘xe5? is a blunder because the a8-rook is defended and after 11...♘xe5 12 ♗xa8 ♘xa8 White is material down with a very weak king.

25) 12 ♘d6+! deflects the b4-bishop, and the black queen is lost after 12...♗xd6 13 ♘xe4.

26) No, because it ignores White's other threat, which is directed against Black's queenside: 11...h6?? (11...♘f6! is safer) 12 ♘xd5! and White wins a piece because 12...♕xd5 13 ♗e4 is a nasty skewer winning the knight on c6, and 12...exd5 leaves the knight *en prise*.

27) Despite being a common move, 7 ♘ge2?? is a fatal mistake because of the simple reply 7...♘g4!. Then 8 0-0 would be a good way to defend f2 were it not for 8...♕h4, adding another attacker while also threatening mate on h2. After 9 h3 ♘xf2 White is getting wiped off the board.

28) The problem with 14 ♘f3? is that Black takes the knight and rather than losing his queen after 14...gxf3 15 ♕xh4 he emerges with an extra rook and knight following 15...fxg2+ 16 ♔f2 gxh1♕. Always check what is happening at the end of the tactic you're looking to execute.

29) 8 ♘g5! simply attacks the f7-pawn, and Black has no good way to defend it. 8...♗xe2 9 ♕xe2 ♘d4 10 ♕d1 leaves the problem of the f7-pawn unsolved, while 8...♗e6 technically saves the pawn for now, but 9 ♘xe6 fxe6 gives Black such a horrible structure and development that it is no better than just giving up the pawn right away.

30) No, a tactic based on promotion wins: 12 fxg7! ♖g8 (12...♘xd4 13 gxh8♕ leaves White a rook up) 13 gxf8♕+ ♔xf8 14 ♕h4 and after 14...♗xg2 15 ♖g1 bxa4 16 ♗g5! Black loses material thanks to 16...♗f3 17 ♗h6+.

31) With 11 c6! the pawn sells its life at a very high cost. This typical *desperado* idea normally just weakens the enemy pawns, but does far more here. After 11...♘c7 12 cxb7 ♘xb5 13 bxc8♕ ♖axc8 14 ♗xb5 White has won a pawn and a piece. 11...♕xc6 12 ♕xc6 bxc6 leaves the a6-knight loose, allowing 13 ♗xa6, while 11...♘h5 12 ♖c1! changes little (12 cxb7?! ♗xc3+ is less clear: 13 ♘d2 ♗xd2+ 14 ♔xd2 ♕d8+ 15 ♔e1 ♘xf4).

32) No, 9...♗xb2?? loses. After 10 fxe5! (10 ♗xf7+? ♔d8 11 fxe5 bxa1♕ 12 ♗xg8, as apparently played by Napoleon, misses the target) 10...bxa1♕ 11 ♕d5 Black is a rook and two pawns up, but his king is defenceless: 11...♘h6 12 ♗xh6 ♖f8 13 ♕xc5 gxh6 14 e6! dxe6 15 ♘a3 ♕g7 16 ♘b5 or 11...♗e7 12 ♕xf7+ ♔d8 13 ♕xg7.

33) 6...♗e7! 7 bxc3 0-0 leaves Black a clear pawn ahead with a good position. This should be enough to win. Instead 6...♗a5? is a greedy attempt to keep a bigger material advantage, but after 7 ♕xg7 Black has a lot of pieces attacked. 7...♘e4+ 8 b4 ♕f6 9 ♕xf6 ♘xf6 10 bxa5 ♘c6 11 ♗d3 also leaves Black a pawn up, but White has space and active play in return.

34) 12...♘xc3?? is a tempting move to insert, as it looks like Black wins a piece after 13 ♗xd8?? ♘e2+ 14 ♔h1 ♘xd4. However, 13 ♕h4! turns the tables. Black will now lose rook for bishop: 13...♘e2+ (13...♕e8 14 bxc3 and ♗xf8) 14 ♔h1 ♕e8 15 ♗xf8 ♕xf8 16 ♖fc1 and the knight is trapped. 12...♕xe7 is the safe, sensible move, leading to roughly equal play after 13 ♘xa4 b6.

35) 13 ♘dxb5! (13 ♘cxb5! works just as well) 13...axb5 14 ♘xb5 knocks the support away from the c4-knight, and 14...♕c6 15 ♕xc4 leaves White two pawns up.

36) With 8 ♗xa7?? White's idea is to exploit Black's *uncompleted fianchetto* after 8...♖xa7?? 9 ♕d4, forking the two rooks. However, 8...b6! traps the bishop and the same double attack, 9 ♕d4, now fails because of 9...e5! 10 ♗xb6 (or 10 ♕xb6 ♖xa7) 10...exd4 11 ♗xc7 dxc3, with an extra piece.

37) True, but after 10 g4! ♘xg4 White needs to play the in-between move 11 ♗d3! (after 11 hxg4 ♗xg4 White has to find 12 ♘e4! to avoid a disadvantage – then White is better, but the game is messy) 11...♕f6 12 ♘e4!, when the queen has no good squares.

38) 12 ♘xd5! wins. The main point is 12...cxd5 13 ♗c7 (a theme that is more familiar when there is a rook on e8, so the queen is simply trapped) 13...♕e8 14 ♕xd5, forking the rook on a8 and the knight on h5. Otherwise, 12...♘xf4 removes the key bishop but allows the sacrificed knight to save its skin by 13 ♘xf4, while after 12...♘c5 13 dxc5 ♗e6 (13...cxd5 leaves White a good pawn up; e.g., 14 ♗d6 ♗xd6 15 ♕xd5) one strong option is 14 ♗c7 intending cxb6.

39) No, 13 ♘dxb5?? axb5 14 ♘xb5 is bad because Black's queen escapes with check, so White doesn't pick up the knight on c4: 14...♕a5+ 15 ♘c3 ♘xe3 and Black wins easily.

40) No, 11...♗xh3?? is bad because of 12 d4!, not only leaving Black with two pieces attacked, but also blocking off the pin of the f2-pawn that is vital to Black's whole idea. White wins a piece.

41) 14...♗d4!! is a double pin or a double deflection, depending on how you look at it. In any case, it is a fantastic move that wins on the spot. After 15 ♖e1 (15 ♕xd4 allows 15...♕xg2#, while 15 ♗xd4 ♘h3+ costs White his queen, and 15 ♘d5 ♘xd5 16 ♕xd4 ♘xe3 is an extra piece for Black) 15...♗xe3+ 16 ♖xe3 ♘xg2! the white queen is overloaded (17 ♕xg2 ♕xe3+), so Black wins a pawn and shatters White's kingside.

42) Yes, because after 11...♕xa2! 12 ♖xa2 bxa2 White has no way to cover the a1-square, so Black gets his queen back, keeping an extra rook.

43) 8...h6?? gets Black in a horrible tangle after 9 ♘xf6+ ♕xf6 10 ♕h7+! ♔f8 11 ♘e4 because 11...♕e7 allows 12 ♕h8#, so Black can't defend his bishop on c5. 8...e4! avoids any invasions on h7, and gives Black very strong play for the pawn after 9 ♘xf6+?! ♕xf6 10 ♘xe4 ♕g6!; e.g., 11 ♗f3 d5! 12 cxd5 ♘e5!.

44) Yes, it is! After 18...♗xe2! 19 ♘g6+ Black avoids mate by playing 19...♕xg6! (White's point was 19...hxg6?? 20 hxg6+, mating) 20 hxg6 ♗xc4!, and wins.

45) Not really. After 11...♗h3?! the bishop can't be taken because 12 ♗xh3?? ♘f3+ is a deadly knight fork, but otherwise the bishop move just wastes time. 12 0-0 is a safe option, while 12 ♘xd4! ♗xg2 13 ♘b3 ♕d8 14 ♖g1 followed by ♕h6 gives White good play.

46) 12 ♖e1! simply pins Black to death. White will regain his piece while keeping an extra pawn. All three pins are important: 12...g6 13 ♕xd5 (e-file); 12...♗e7 13 ♖xe6 (h5-e8 diagonal); 12...♘c7 13 ♗xe6 (a2-g8 diagonal) 13...♘xe6 14 ♖xe6+. After 12...♘f6 13 ♖xe6+ ♗e7 White wins thanks to a discovered attack on f7: 14 ♖xf6! gxf6 15 ♕xf7+ ♔d7 16 ♗f4 with decisive threats.

47) Yes, 12 a3! wins a piece. The main point is that after 12...♗a5 13 ♗d2 the pin is far more effective.

48) False, because 13...♘fxe4!! overloads the queen. After 14 fxe4 ♗xd4+ 15 ♕xd4 (or 15 ♔h1 ♗xc3! 16 bxc3 ♘xe4) 15...♕xg5 Black is a good pawn ahead. 14 ♘xe4 ♘xe4 15 fxe4 ♗xd4+ is similar, while 14 ♗xd8 ♘xd2 is also winning for Black.

49) After 15 ♕b6+! axb6 16 ♗xb6+ ♔e8 17 ♘c7+ ♔d8 White has no instant mate, but can clean up most of Black's pieces with repeated checks and discovered checks: 18 ♘xa8+ ♔e8 19 ♘c7+ ♔d8 20 ♘xe6++ ♔e8 21 ♘c7+ ♔d8 22 ♘d5+ ♔e8 23 ♖e1+ and Black will have to give up at least two more pieces.

50) 15 ♗d3?? might seem like the safe and sensible move, developing a piece, but it is a terrible mistake because the fork trick 15...♕xd3+! 16 ♔xd3 ♘xf2+ 17 ♔e2 ♘xg4 leaves Black two pawns up. 15 ♔xe4! looks risky but wins, because the king is safe in the middle of the board since Black can't bring in pieces to attack it. 15...0-0 threatens ...f5+, but 16 ♗f6 is one good answer, as is 16 ♕f5.

51) The pawn-thrust 11 e6! is clearly a good idea, even if you can't calculate the lines to a finish. 11...fxe6? 12 ♗g6+ and 11...♕xe6 12 ♖e1 both cost Black his queen, and seeing this is enough to decide upon 11 e6, since after 11...♕c7 12 exf7+ ♔xf7 White has clearly worsened Black's position considerably. One game continued 13 ♖e1!? (the simple 13 ♗h4 is also very good for White, as the black king will not find safety) 13...hxg5?! 14 ♘xg5+ ♔f6 (or 14...♔g8 15 ♗h7+ ♖xh7 16 ♕xd5+ ♔h8 17 ♘f7+) 15 ♘h7+ ♖xh7 16 ♕f3+, winning.

52) The only good reply is to give up the queen with 10...axb5! 11 axb6 ♖xa1+ 12 ♔e2 ♘xb6, when Black is winning! He has more or less enough material for the queen, and is dominating the queenside while White can't develop his kingside. It's a classic case of *winning the queen for too much*. One game ended 13 b3 c4 14 ♔e3 h6 15 ♗h4 g5 16 ♗g3 ♗b4 17 c3 ♗a3 18 ♕c2 ♖c1 0-1.

53) 12 exd5! opens the e-file with deadly effect. 12...♕xd5? and 12...♗xd5? both lose the knight due to 13 ♕xf6, while 12...♘xd5 13 c4 ♘b4 14 d5 ♗d7 15 ♗g5 is a bind from which Black will never escape.

54) Instead of 14 ♕xd4??, White wins with 14 ♔h1! since 14...f6 is illegal, and 14...♕b6 15 ♗e7 is hopeless for Black.

55) No. After 14 ♘e4? the best reply is 14...♕xd5!, when White can win the *queen*, but that isn't the same as *winning material*! 15 ♘f6+ gxf6 16 ♗xd5 ♗xd5 gives Black three well-coordinated and secure pieces, which are worth more than a queen. Black has extremely good winning chances.

56) Yes, 10 ♘c4! wins a piece because 10...♘xd1+ 11 ♘xa5 leaves the knight trapped on d1. Black can try 10...♕xd5 11 bxc3 ♕xg2, when he gets three pawns for the piece, but in a middlegame with poor development this is not enough; e.g., 12 ♗f3 ♕h3 13 ♖b1 and Black's position will soon crack. As for 10 bxc3?!, it is only a little better for White after 10...♕xc3+ or 10...dxe5.

57) False. After 10 ♘f5? exf5 11 ♗d4 Black walks into the trap with 11...♕xd4! 12 ♗b5+ axb5 13 ♕xd4 ♘f6 and, with three pieces for a queen, is simply better.

58) 12 ♗xb5! exploits the fact that the black queen must cover d8 and that the d6-knight is tied to defending f7. As well as grabbing a pawn, the bishop move adds the threat of ♕xe6+ to the mix. After 12...g5 the simplest win is 13 ♕xe6+ ♔d8 14 ♕xg8, while 12...♗d5 13 ♘d2!? intends ♘e4, as the d5-bishop is now overloaded! And after 12...♘c6 13 ♗xc6 ♗xc6 14 ♘xc6 Black can't take the knight.

59) The queen sacrifice 8 ♘xe5! ♗xd1 9 ♗b5+ creates such strong threats against the black king that White wins back more than enough material: 9...c6 10 dxc6 ♗g4 (no better are 10...a6 11 c7+, 10...♕b8 11 c7+ and 10...♕b6 11 cxb7+) 11 ♘xg4 bxc6 12 ♗xc6+ ♘d7 13 ♘e5 ♕c7 14 ♗xd7+ ♔d8 15 ♗f4 gives White three pieces and a massive attack for the queen.

60) It all becomes clear if Black plays 10...dxc5??: 11 ♘xh7! ♖xh7 12 ♗xg6+ ♔f8 and with the d-file open, White can take the black queen.

61) 11 ♕f2?? is a terrible mistake because of 11...♘xe4! (11...♘g4? 12 ♕e2 is far less clear), when both 12 ♘xe4 ♗xd4 and 12 ♗xc4 ♗xd4 leave the white queen pinned and lost. 11 ♘e2 is the right move, and gives White a good game.

62) 9...d5? allows the target to escape with 10 e5. 9...♘xe4! wins a pawn since Black will be able to attack e4 with his d- or f-pawn: 10 ♗xe4 (10 ♘xe4? d5 will cost White even more material) 10...d5 (10...f5 is also good) and 11...dxe4 will give Black a good extra pawn since 11 ♘xd5? ♛xe4+ 12 ♛xe4 ♖xe4+ 13 ♘e2 ♝g4 14 ♘c3 ♖e7! leaves White's king and knights in a deadly crossfire from all the black pieces.

63) 9 ♗xb7! has the idea of deflecting the black bishop from controlling f5, so White can give a deadly queen check. Black is mated or loses a lot of material: 9...♗xb7 10 ♛f5+ ♚h6 11 d4+ g5 12 ♗xg5+ and the black queen is lost, while 9...♝d6 is met by 10 ♛a5!, simply maintaining the ♛f5+ idea.

64) 12...d6?? is a blunder because of 13 ♖xe7+! ♚xe7 14 cxd6+. 12...d5 is Black's best move because the *en passant* capture can only be made immediately, and not delayed a move: thus 13 ♖xe7+? ♚xe7 offers White nothing because 14 cxd6+ is illegal here, while 13 cxd6?? blunders the white queen.

65) Because 11 b4? allows 11...♘xb4! 12 axb4 ♗xb4, when the pin on the c3-knight enables Black to regain the piece with a huge advantage: 13 ♗e5 (or 13 ♖c1 e5! 14 ♗xe5 ♖xe5! 15 ♘xe5 ♘e4) 13...♘e4 14 ♖c1 f6 15 ♗d3 (15 ♗d4? e5) 15...fxe5 16 ♗xe4 dxe4 is about the best White can do, but he will be a pawn down and solidly worse.

66) First of all, don't panic! Never assume you have fallen into a trap just because the opponent has created an unexpected threat. 7...♚f8! is the first step, so that the knight doesn't fork king and rook. If White has to retreat, then he will have lost time too. And if he persists with 8 ♘c7?, then Black gets a big advantage with 8...e5!, cutting off the knight's support: 9 ♘xe5 (after 9 ♘xa8 exf4 the knight will be trapped on a8) 9...♗xe5! (not 9...♘xe5? 10 ♘xa8 ♘c6 11 c3, when the knight escapes via c7) 10 ♗xe5 (10 dxe5 ♛xc7) 10...♘xe5 11 ♘xa8 ♘c6 and Black will round up the knight by ...♗e6 and ...♛xa8.

67) By using a standard theme with a skewer and a double attack: 12 ♘xd5! ♛xd5 (or 12...exd5 13 ♛c2) 13 ♗e4 ♛d6 14 ♛c2 and Black must save his knight, leaving the h7-pawn to be taken.

68) Certainly not, as 12 ♘d5! wins thanks to threats of both mate and a knight fork on e7: 12...♗xd4 (12...e5 13 ♛xe4 leaves Black a piece down) 13 ♘xe7+ ♚g7 and the fact that 14 ♗xd4+ is check means that Black loses material.

69) Black is trying to exploit White's *uncompleted fianchetto*, but after 12 ♛xg4! ♛xh1 he is too far behind in development: 13 ♛a4+! (13 0-0-0? ♛c6 is safe for Black) 13...b5 (13...♛c6 14 ♗b5 and 13...♚d8 14 0-0-0+ are just as bad) 14 ♘xb5! 0-0-0 (14...axb5 15 ♛xb5+ ♚d8 16 ♖d1+ gives White a mating attack) and now the cleanest kill is 15 ♛c4+!, mating quickly.

70) White must strike now to exploit Black's backward development. 14 e6! is fairly obvious, but White needed to see the follow-up after 14...f6 (14...♖g8 15 ♛a4+ is similar). 15 f5? is tempting in view of 15...♗xf5?? 16 ♖xf5 gxf5 17 ♗h5#, but Black doesn't have to take, and 15...♗g7 gives him a playable game. The right path is 15 ♛a4+! (15 ♗xa6! is also good) 15...♖c6 (15...b5? 16 ♗xb5+ leads to mate) 16 ♗xa6!! and White wins material: 16...♛c8 (16...bxa6? 17 ♛xc6+ and mate next move; 16...♗xc2 17 b3) 17 ♗b5. Instead 14 ♗xa6?! is a less accurate move-order, since 14...bxa6 15 e6 ♛d6 is not so clear-cut.

71) 20 ♛f4+! not only regains a piece, but opens a way in for White's rook: 20...♗f6 (20...♚g7? allows mate in two) 21 exf6 exf6 22 ♚d2 (or 22 ♚f1) intending ♖e1 with decisive

74

threats. Instead the tempting 20 Qg6? is a misfire because 20...Qd5 parries the mate threat and leaves the game unclear. After 21 Qe8+ Kg7 22 Qxe7+ Kg8 23 Qe8+ Kg7 White may have nothing better than a draw by perpetual check since 24 Qxc8 Qd7 will lead to an unclear ending.

72) There is no need to retreat the knight, as opening the h-file gives White a decisive attack: 14 hxg6! exd4 (14...hxg6 15 Bxg7 Kxg7 16 Qh6+ Kg8 17 Qh8#; 14...fxg6 15 Bc4+ Kh8 16 Bxg7+ Kxg7 17 Ne6+ Nxe6 18 Bxe6 and White will win a pawn on either d6 or g6 and dominates the board) 15 gxh7+ Kh8 (15...Nxh7 16 Bxg7 Qg5 17 Qxg5 Nxg5 18 Bxd4 leaves White two pawns up) 16 Bxg7+ Kxg7 17 h8Q+! (not 17 Qh6+?? Kh8, when Black is winning!) 17...Kxh8 18 Qg5+ Kf8 19 Rxh8+ and Black loses the house.

73) Yes, since Black only threatens to win a pawn, whereas 10 Ba6! wins a whole piece. After 10...Qxh2+ 11 Kf1, both 11...bxa6 12 Qxc6+, intending Qxa8, and 11...Ne7 12 Bxb7 0-0 13 Bxc6 leave White material up, while 11...0-0-0 12 Qxc6 bxa6 13 Be3 gives White a decisive attack on the black king; e.g., 13...Ne7 14 Qxa6+ Kd7 15 Qa4+ Nc6 (15...Kc8 16 Nb5) 16 Rac1 with too many threats, including Ne4.

74) 10 Bc5!! combines a pin with a snap mate idea. The bishop can't be taken because 10...dxe5 11 Nc7# is mate, while after 10...Nxd1 11 Bxb2 Nxb2 12 Nc7+ Kd8 13 Nxa8 White is material up and trapping the knight on b2.

75) After 10...Qb6! the X-ray attack through to b2 and the threat of ...Bxc3 expose all the weak spots of White's position. 11 a4 a6 12 a5 Qb7 solves nothing for White, while 11 Rb1 Bxc3 12 bxc3 a6 13 Qh6 f6! gives Black an extra piece. 11 Qd3 a6 12 Bc4 Qxb2 creates a fatal double attack on a1 and c3, as 13 Kd2 Bf5 ties White up even more: 14 Ne4 (14 Rab1 Bxd3 15 Rxb2 Bxc4) 14...Qb4+ 15 c3 Qb2+ 16 Ke3 Bh6+ is a knockout.

76) No, because the f6-knight can be exchanged and the e6-bishop pinned, leaving the queen loose. How do these miracles happen? With 12 Nxe5! dxe5 13 Nxf6+ gxf6 14 Qxd7.

77) 10 Re1? overlooks 10...Nxd4!, winning a pawn. The key point is that after 11 Bxd7 Black inserts 11...Nxf3+ before recapturing the bishop on d7. This is a typical tactic that arises in many openings. 11 Nxd4 cxd4 12 Bxd7 dxc3 and 11 exd4 Bxb5 also give Black a safe extra pawn. Instead 10 a4 is a useful move that stakes out space on the queenside. It also parries Black's threat of taking on d4 by protecting the bishop.

78) No. It looks like White has just been punished for his slow development and weak back rank, but there is a way out for him. 17 Bxb7+! makes a square for his king with gain of time, and after 17...Kxb7 18 Nxa2 Rd1+ 19 Kg2 Rxh1 20 Kxh1 material is level and White is no worse.

79) 5 Nxe5! is a *Sicilian unpin*. It wins a pawn, but you need to have checked that 5...Bxe2 6 Nxc6 Qf6 wasn't a problem. White wins with 7 Qxe2 Qxa1 8 Qb5! Qxb1 9 Ne5+ c6 10 Qxb7! Be7 (or 10...Qxc1+ 11 Ke2 Qxh1 12 Qd7#) 11 Qxc6+.

80) Your task here was to avoid the blunder! 11 Nxc3?? is a terrible mistake, as Black wins with 11...Rxb2! 12 Bxb2 Bxc3+ 13 Bxc3 Qxc3+ 14 Ke2 Ba6+. Instead 11 Qd2! followed by Nxc3 safely wins a piece. 11 bxc3 is also good.

81) Yes, 8 dxc6! catches Black in a well-known opening trap. 8...Nxc6 9 Rxb1 leaves White a pawn up with a good position, and 8...Be4? loses to the spectacular 9 Rxa7!! Rxa7 10 c7, when the pawn promotes. This idea is better known with White's centre pawns arranged a little differently, but that makes no difference to the tactic working.

82) No, because after 12...Nxd4? 13 Nxd4 Qxd4 he has walked into a devastating discovered attack: 14 Nd5! Qc5 15 Bxf6 and after 15...Bxf6 16 Qe4! Black can only avoid mate at a huge cost in material: 16...g6 17 Nxf6+ Kg7 18 Qxb7. 15...gxf6 is no better: 16 Nxe7+ Qxe7 17 Qg4+!! (17 Qh5? f5) 17...Kh8 18 Qh4 and because the f6-pawn is pinned, Black must lose his queen to prevent Qxh7#.

83) 9 Ne5! is a standard long-diagonal pin theme (9 Ng5?! Nc3! gives Black more hope of surviving). 9...Nd6 (9...Nxd2 is hopeless: 10 Bxb7 Qc7 11 Bxa8 Nxf1 12 Qxf1 Qxe5 13 Bf4) 10 Bxb7 Nxb7 and now White has various strong options, the clearest win being 11 Qf3!, attacking f7 and b7. After 11...Qc7 12 Ne4!! (threatening Bf4 or Ng5) 12...Qxe5 13 Bf4 Qd5 (trying to cover the long diagonal; 13...Qxb2 14 Ng5 and 13...Qf5 14 Nc3 intend Qxb7) 14 Rad1 Qc6 15 Bxb8! Rxb8 16 Nf6+ the black queen is lost.

84) With the right follow-up 12 Nxe5! does indeed win a pawn. 12...Nxg3 is answered with the *desperado* 13 Nxc6 bxc6 14 hxg3, with an extra pawn, while after 12...Nxe5 White must avoid the queen trap 13 Qxh5?? Bg4, and insert 13 Bxe5! dxe5 before playing 14 Qxh5.

85) 17 Nf6+! is a standard and decisive sacrifice. After 17...gxf6 18 Qg4+ Kh8 19 exf6 (not 19 Qh4? f5) 19...Rg8 (19...Bxf6 20 Qh5 and mate on h7) 20 Qh4 Black can only avoid mate at a catastrophic material cost. Declining is also hopeless; the loose pieces on a5 and d7 make the variations straightforward: 17...Kh8 loses to 18 Qd3 g6 19 Qxd7, and 17...Bxf6 18 exf6 Rfc8 (18...Rfe8 19 Qg4 g6 20 Qg5 and 18...Qc5 19 Qd3 Qf5 20 Qd1 both cost Black a piece, while 18...Bc6 19 Bxh7+ Kxh7 20 Qh5+ Kg8 21 Qg5 mates) 19 Bxh7+! Kf8 20 Nd5! gives White an overwhelming attack.

86) 14 Re5! is a key setting-up move, forcing the black queen to d3. 14...Qd3 (14...Qg4 15 h3) 15 Rxe7+! Kxe7 (or 15...Kf8 16 Rxf7+) 16 Nxd5+ is a deadly discovered attack. After 16...Nxd5 17 Qxd3 White is material up with the black king in a mess.

87) 11...Nxd4?? has the point that after White takes on d4, 12...Ba4 traps the white queen thanks to the pin on the c3-knight. Indeed 12 exd4?? Ba4 13 Bc7 b6 is winning for Black. However, 12 Nxd4! Ba4 13 Qxa4+ Qxa4 14 Bb5+ Qxb5 15 Nxb5 turns it into an exchange of queens and leaves White a piece up.

88) No, 12 Bxf7+? Kxf7 13 Qc4+ doesn't work because the king is safe after 13...Kg6!. White can't play Nh4+, and the mate threat after 14 Ng5 is easily parried; e.g., 14...Bd8 intending ...h6. So the simple 12 Ng5! is best, when 12...Ne6 13 Nxe6 Bxe6 14 Bxe6 fxe6 leaves Black with weak pawns.

89) No. 14...Bh3? has a nice idea behind it: 15 Bxh3?? Nxe4 16 Qf4 Qa5+ and Black wins back the piece with a big advantage unless White tries 17 b4 Qxb4+ 18 Kf1 f5 but Black's huge swathe of pawns makes that appalling for White. 15 Bf3? avoids material loss but after 15...e5 White can't complete his development and his king is terribly placed. However, 15 Bxf6! refutes Black's plan: 15...Bxg2 16 Bxg7 Kxg7 (16...Bxh1 17 Bxf8 followed by Qxd4 also leaves White a pawn up) 17 Rg1 and White will be a pawn up after taking on d4 since 17...Bxe4?? loses to 18 Qxd4+. There is a danger of being too caught up working out

76

nice tactical lines after 15 ♗xh3?? that we forget to check if there is some other move that turns the tables completely.

90) White has several good options here, but 12 e6! is best, and should win. After 12...fxe6 13 ♘e5 Black can't defend on his light squares: 13...♕f6 (13...♗xb5? 14 ♕h5+ ♔e7 15 ♕f7+ ♔d6 16 dxc5+ ♖xc5 17 ♗xc5+ ♔xc5 18 ♕xb7 and a rook check on c1; 13...♘f6 14 ♕b1!; 13...g6 14 ♗d3) 14 ♘xd7 ♘xd7 15 dxc5 with equal material and very strong threats for White. And 12...♗xb5 13 exf7+ ♔xf7 14 ♘e5+ ♔e6 leads to a king-hunt, with many ways for White to win; e.g., 15 ♕g4+ ♔f6 16 ♕g6+ ♔e7 17 ♕f7+ ♔d6 18 ♗f4 (or 18 dxc5+!) 18...♖c7 19 ♘d7+ ♔c6 20 ♕e6+ ♔d6 21 ♕xd6#.

91) 9 ♗xf7+! ♔xf7 10 ♘e6! is a standard theme that you may have seen in a famous game by Fischer. After 10...♔xe6 11 ♕c4+ d5 12 exd5+! ♔f7 (12...♔d6? 13 ♘b5+ ♔e5 14 ♖e1+ ♔f5 15 ♕d3+ mates) 13 d6+ White wins because there is the additional idea of using the pawn to trap the black queen: 13...♘d5 (13...♔f8 14 dxc7 and the queen is lost!) 14 dxe7 (not 14 dxc7?? ♕xc7) 14...♕xe7 15 ♘xd5 and White emerges at least two pawns up.

92) 13 ♗xh6! d6 (hoping to defend with ...♗f5; 13...gxh6 14 ♕g6 leaves Black powerless against ♘f6 or ♕xh6+ followed by ♘g5) and of several options, 14 ♕g6! ♕d7 (14...gxh6 15 ♕xh6+ ♔g8 16 ♘f6+) 15 ♘g5 is one good way to win: 15...gxh6 16 ♕xh6+ ♔g8 17 ♘f6+ ♖xf6 18 exf6.

93) 9...♘xa2! traps White's bishop on c1 and exploits the overloaded rook on a1. 10 b4 gives Black a pleasant choice between 10...♘xb4 and 10...♘xc1 11 ♕b2 ♘xe2, when 12 ♔xe2 leaves the white king absurdly placed, while 12 ♗xe2 ♕xg2 will give Black a big material advantage: bishop and four good pawns for a rook. 10 b3 is similar, while 10 ♕d4 ♘xc1 and 10 e3 ♘xc1 leave White heavily down on material. 10 ♔d1 fails to protect the bishop: 10...♗e6 11 e3 ♘xc1 12 ♕c3 ♘b3.

94) I hope you didn't choose 11...♗d7??, as Black did in one game, as it is mated by 12 ♘d6#. Black does far better to allow White's idea since after 11...axb5! 12 ♗c3 ♗d7 13 ♗xh8 ♖xa2! he is winning! The white king is in deep trouble, while the h8-bishop is in danger of being trapped, but more importantly shut out from defending its king, by ...f6. For example, 14 ♗d3 ♕a5 15 c3 (15 ♗c3 b4 and the bishop has no better square than returning to h8!) 15...f6.

95) 12 ♗xf7+! is an idea we have seen in other positions as a way to trap the queen or mate the king. Here it is more directed against the loose bishop on g5. 12...♖xf7 (12...♔xf7 can be answered simply with 13 ♕h5+ or more devastatingly by 13 ♘e6! ♔xe6 14 ♕d5+ ♔e7 15 ♗xg5+ ♘f6 16 ♕xa8) 13 ♘e6! and after 13...♕e7 14 ♘xg5 Black must give up rook for knight since 14...♖f8? 15 ♕d5+ costs him the other rook in the corner.

96) After 13...♖d8? White replies 14 ♖d5!, when the tactics work in his favour: 14...♕xf4? allows 15 ♖xd8+, while 14...♘xd5 15 ♗c7 ♘xc7 does not give Black enough for the queen. 14...♖xd5 15 ♘xd5 ♕b7 16 ♘xe7+ ♕xe7 17 ♗xc6 shows us a major theme: trapping the black rook in the corner. 14...e5 limits the damage to a pawn, but a very good one: 15 ♖xd8+ ♕xd8 (15...♗xd8 16 ♗xe5!) 16 ♕xd8+ ♗xd8 17 ♗xe5. And 14...♕b6 15 ♖xd8+ brings in more trapping themes: 15...♗xd8 16 ♘a4! ♕a5 17 b4 runs the queen out of squares where it can defend the bishop, while 15...♕xd8 allows the trapping of the rook: 16 ♕xd8+ ♗xd8 17 ♗xc6 ♖a7 18 ♖d1 ♗a5 (18...♗e7 19 ♗b8) 19 ♗e3 ♖e7 20 ♗c5.

6 Hunting the King

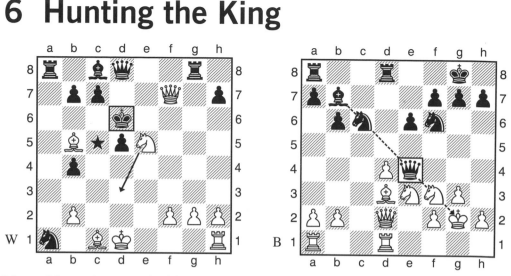

Many of the tactics we see in this book have the goal of ripping the enemy king away from its bodyguards and mating it. But what if there is no instant mate and the king can run for its life across the board? Will it reach safety or will our pieces hunt it down? This is our topic in this short but exciting chapter. A good feel for when a king is safe, and when it is not, will help greatly when assessing all sorts of sacrificial ideas.

In a king-hunt, don't assume you need to chase the king with constant checks. Sometimes a 'quiet' move is needed. In our first diagram, a knight retreat seals the king's fate: 17 ♘d3! covers the flight-square c5 and prepares ♗f4+. There's no reply; e.g., 17...♖g4 18 ♗f4+ (18 ♖e1 is also strong) 18...♖xf4 19 ♕xf4+ ♔e7 20 ♕g5+ ♔f7 21 ♘e5+ and Black loses his queen.

In the second position above, Black's queen is trapped. But he needn't be too upset, because he can sacrifice it and start a decisive king-hunt: 16...♕xf3+! 17 ♔xf3 ♘xd4++ 18 ♔f4 e5+! 19 ♔xe5 ♘f3+. Once Black had seen this far, he could have relaxed, seeing that he could regain the queen and so was risking nothing by going in for this line. This is an important point: we can use 'stepping stones' like this to help our calculation. We can safely play the first few moves, and if we then find nothing better than regaining material or giving perpetual check, we have a way to bail out and avoid losing. In fact, Black has a forced mate here: 20 ♔f4 g5+ 21 ♔f5 ♗c8+ 22 ♔xf6 ♖d6+ 23 ♔e7 ♖e6+ 24 ♔d8 ♗a6+ 25 ♔c7 ♖c8+ 26 ♔d7 ♘e5#, and after 20 ♔f5, out of many strong continuations, the nicest mate is 20...g6+ 21 ♔xf6 ♖d6+ 22 ♔e7 ♖e6+ 23 ♔d7 ♘e5+ 24 ♔c7 ♖e7+ 25 ♔d6 ♔f8! intending ...♖d8#.

- Don't assume that a king in the middle of the board is doomed. You have probably sacrificed to drag the king out, so your remaining pieces will have to work quickly and efficiently. In your calculations, remember that you don't have the pieces you sacrificed any more!
- Once the enemy king is on its fourth rank, your pawns are likely to play a role in the attack.
- Be on the lookout for counter-sacrifices (i.e. the defender giving back some or all of the material). Any move that offers the king a route to safety should be considered.

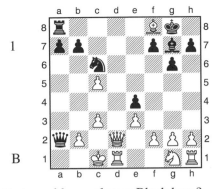

1

B

What would you play as Black here?

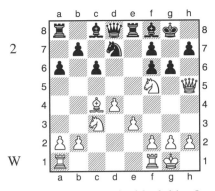

2

W

How do you root out the black king?

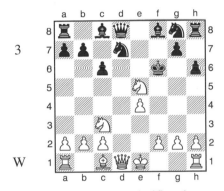

3

W

A multi-purpose move clarifies the game in White's favour.

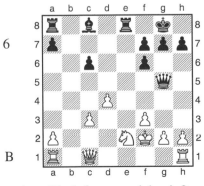

4

B

How do you round off Black's king-hunt?

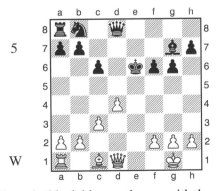

5

W

Keep the black king on the run with the right queen check.

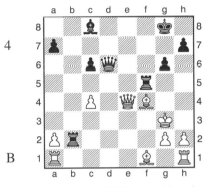

6

B

How does Black force a quick win?

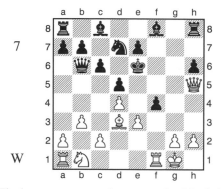

7

Find a pawn move that stops the black king from fleeing to safety on the queenside.

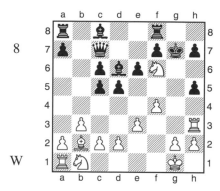

8

How do you drive the king up the board and force a quick mate?

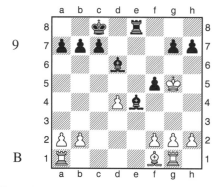

9

How do you finish off the white king?

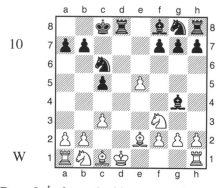

10

Does 9 ♔c2 put the king on a safe square?

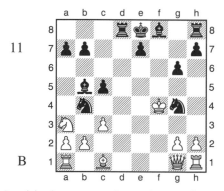

11

A critical moment. A good move is needed to make sure the white king doesn't escape.

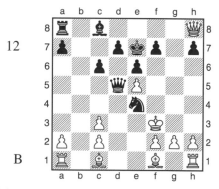

12

Black has lots of checks, but only one that is any good. Can you find it?

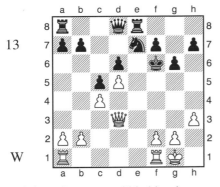

13

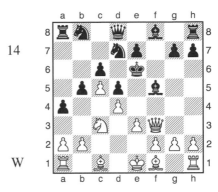

14

Black is a piece up and his king is one move away from safety. What should White play?

A piece down, White must create threats against the black king right away.

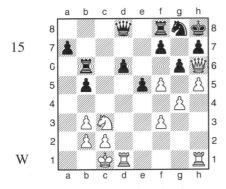

15

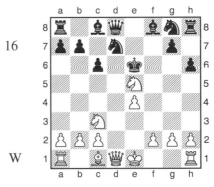

16

White forces a spectacular checkmate.

Black's king is on the run. Choose between 9 ♕g4+ and 9 f4.

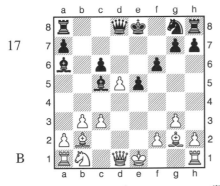

17

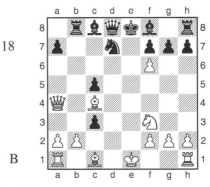

18

Choose between 11...♗xf2+ and 11...♕b6.

Black's best move here is 12...♖b4. What is wrong with 12...cxb2?

Solutions to Hunting the King Exercises

1) There's a forced mate in five moves: 14...♕a1+ 15 ♔c2 ♘b4+! 16 ♔b3 (16 cxb4 ♕xb2#) 16...♕a2+ 17 ♔xb4 a5+ 18 ♔b5 ♕b3#.

2) The bishop sacrifice 13 ♗xf7+! sends the king on a one-way journey up the middle of the board: 13...♔xf7 14 ♕xh7+ ♔e6 15 ♕g8+ ♔xf5 16 g4+! and the king will soon be mated: 16...♔xg4 (16...♔g5 17 f4+) 17 ♕xg6+ ♔h4 18 ♕h7+ and now either 18...♔g5 19 f4+ ♔g4 20 h3+ ♔g3 21 ♘e2# or 18...♔g4 19 h3+ ♔g5 20 f4#.

3) 9 ♕d4!! prevents ...♔xe5, maintains the pin on the d7-knight, and threatens ♘xd7++. Then 9...c5 does nothing to prevent 10 ♘xd7++ because this is a *double* check. 9...♔e6 avoids that problem, but invites 10 ♘g6 ♖h7 11 ♕c4+ ♔f6 12 ♘f4 threatening both ♕xg8 and ♕e6+, mating.

4) 22...♖g5+! uses the pin to force a quick mate or win of the white queen: 23 ♔f3 (23 ♔h4 ♖g4+ 24 ♔h3 ♖xf4+) 23...♗g4+! 24 ♔g3 (24 ♔e3 ♕d2#) 24...♗f5+.

5) 15 ♕b3+! is best because the king must come up the board. 15...♔f5 (15...♔e7 16 ♗f4 threatens ♖e1+; 15...♔d6 invites 16 ♗f4+, and 15...♔d7 loses the rook in the corner: 16 ♕xb7+ ♕c7 17 ♕xa8) and of several good moves, 16 f3! threatens g4#, and there's no good answer: 16...h5 17 g4+ hxg4 18 fxg4+ ♔e4 (18...♔xg4 19 ♕e6+ f5 20 ♕xg6+ ♔h4 21 ♗e3 leads to mate) 19 ♕e6+ forces mate with checks: 19...♔f3 20 ♕e3+ ♔xg4 21 ♕f4+ ♔h5 22 ♕f3+ ♔h4 23 ♕g3+ ♔h5 24 ♕h3#.

6) 15...♖xe2+! 16 ♔xe2 ♕xg2+ starts a king-hunt that will end in mate: 17 ♔d3 (or 17 ♔e3 ♗a6 intending ...♖e8+) 17...♗f5+ 18 ♔c4 ♕e2+ 19 ♔c5 (19 ♔b4 ♖b8+) 19...♕b5+ 20 ♔d6 ♕d5+ 21 ♔c7 ♕d7#.

7) Black is intending ...♔d6 and ...♔c7, and 15 c4! prevents this because of the pawn fork on c5. Black is then in deep trouble: 15...♖g8 (15...♔d6? 16 c5+ ♘xc5 17 ♕e5+, etc.; 15...dxc4 16 bxc4 ♕b2 17 c5! threatens to mate) 16 ♕f5+ ♔d6 17 ♕xf4+! (not 17 c5+? ♘xc5 18 ♕e5+ ♔d7 19 ♗f5+ ♔d8, when Black is safe) 17...e5 18 c5+! ♘xc5 19 ♕xe5+ ♔d7 20 ♖f7+ ♔d8 21 ♕f6+ and Black will soon be mated.

8) The double check 15 ♘e8++! forces the king to advance since 15...♔g8 16 ♖g3# is instant mate, and after 15...♔h6 the key point is the bishop check 16 ♗g7+!, when 16...♔g6 17 ♖g3+ ♔f5 18 ♖g5+ ♔e4 19 ♘c3# rounds things off nicely.

9) The rook-lift 18...♖e6! will force the white king to the edge of the board, and the bishops will then take the rest of its squares from it: 19 ♗e2 ♖g6+ 20 ♔h4 ♗f4 21 ♗h5 ♖h6 22 g4 g5+ 23 ♔h3 ♗f3! with mate soon to come. 19 g4 ♖g6+ 20 ♔h4 ♗f4 21 g5 h6 22 ♔h5 ♖d6 23 g6 avoids instant mate, but 23...♗xh2 corners the white rook.

10) In this queenside structure the king is often well-placed on c2, but in this particular position 9 ♔c2?? allows a vicious king-hunt: 9...♗f5+! 10 ♔b3 c4+! (not 10...♘a5+? 11 ♔a3!? c4+ 12 b4 cxb3+ 13 ♔b2 bxa2 14 ♖xa2, when White has good queenside play). Then 11 ♗xc4 ♘a5+ costs White his bishop, 11 ♔xc4 ♗e6+ 12 ♔b5 ♖d5+ is mate after 13 ♔c4 ♘a5# or 13 ♔a4 ♖a5#, while 11 ♔a4 ♗c2+ 12 b3 (12 ♔b5 ♖d5+ 13 ♔xc4 ♖c5#) 12...♖d5 leads to mate next move.

11) The light-squared bishop and the g4-knight are key pieces in the pursuit of the king, and 17...♗e2! keeps them both. The threats include ...♖d3 and ...♗h6+. 18 cxb4 ♖d3 (18...♗h6+

19 ♔g3 ♖d3+ 20 ♔h4 g5+ is also good; e.g., 21 ♔h5 ♖g8 intending 22...♘f6+ 23 ♔xh6 ♖g6#) 19 h3 (or 19 ♕xc5 e5+) 19...♗h6+ 20 ♔e4 ♘f6+ 21 ♔e5 ♖d5+ 22 ♔e6 ♗d3 and mate follows with 23...♖d6+ 24 ♔e5 ♘d7#. Other 17th moves are ineffective: 17...h5? 18 ♘xb5 leaves the king safe on the light squares, while 17...♗d7? 18 cxb4 is far from clear.

12) 13...♘f6+! is the winning move. The point is to cut the white queen off from e5 so the black queen can take the pawn and the knight can then give check, discovering an attack on the white queen: 14 ♔g3 ♕xe5+ 15 f4 (15 ♔h3 allows mate by 15...♕h5+ 16 ♔g3 ♕g4#) and now 15...♘h5+ or 15...♘e4+ wins the white queen. Otherwise, 14 ♔e3 ♕xe5+ 15 ♔d2 ♘e4+ picks off the queen, and 14 ♔f4 ♕e4+ 15 ♔g5 ♕f5+ mates next move. 14 ♔e2 walks into an additional ingredient: the bishop check 14...♗a6+ discovers an attack from the a8-rook.

13) After the obvious 18 ♕c3+ ♔g5, the key move is 19 ♕g7!, denying the king a route back. White will now mate with a little help from his kingside pawns; e.g., 19...♖g8 20 f4+ ♔f5 21 g4+ ♔e4 22 ♖ae1+ ♔d3 23 ♕c3# or 19...♘f5 20 f4+ ♔h5 21 ♕xh7+ ♘h6 22 g4+ ♔h4 23 ♕xh6+ ♔g3 24 ♖ad1 ♗e3 25 ♖d2.

14) 12 g4! is best. 12...♗g6 13 g5! (threatening to mate with ♗h3+) 13...♗f5 14 ♗g2!? threatens 15 ♕xd5+! cxd5 16 ♗xd5#, and Black must give away his d7-knight to prevent this. 12...♗c2 is answered with 13 e4! (threatening ♕f5# now that the bishop is not covering that square) 13...♘f6 14 exd5+ and ♕e2+ will win the black bishop. Instead 12 ♗xb5? ♘f6 (avoiding 12...cxb5?? 13 ♕xd5+) 13 ♗xa4 gives White three pawns for the piece, but leaves the black king safe.

15) I hope you had seen the variation to the end before deciding to sacrifice your queen: 20 ♕xh7+!! ♔xh7 21 hxg6++ ♔g7 22 ♖h7+ ♔f6 23 ♘d5+ ♔g5 24 ♖h5#. The knight, rook and pawns do an amazing job covering all the key squares.

16) 9 ♕g4+? is a case of *over-sacrificing*. It is tempting to force the king to a centre square, but after 9...♔xe5 White doesn't have enough active pieces to prevent the king from returning to safety. For instance, 10 ♕f5+ (10 ♕g6 ♘gf6; 10 ♗f4+ ♔f6 11 ♕f5+ ♔e7) 10...♔d6 11 ♗f4+ ♔e7 12 0-0-0 ♕c8 13 ♗d6+ ♔d8 14 ♗xf8 ♘e7, still with one extra piece. 9 f4! is a good move. White is only a little material down and keeps strong threats against the black king. The knight on e5 is a mighty powerful piece and shouldn't be given away without careful calculation. White threatens ♕g4+ and ♘g6, as well as simply continuing developing. Black will not be able to solve his many problems.

17) 11...♕b6? is easily met by 12 ♕c2, so Black needs to sacrifice to get at White's king here: 11...♗xf2+! 12 ♔xf2 ♕b6+ forces White's king into no man's land: 13 ♔f3 (13 ♔e1? ♕e3+ 14 ♕e2 ♕xe2#) 13...e4+! 14 ♔xe4 ♕f2! and the king will perish mid-board; e.g., 15 c4 ♕xg2+ and ...♕xb2; 15 ♕f3 cxd5+! 16 ♔xd5 ♖d8+ 17 ♔e4 ♗b7+; 15 ♗f3 0-0-0, etc.; 15 ♕e1 cxd5+ 16 ♔xd5+ ♘e7+, etc.

18) After 12...cxb2? something dramatic is needed, so I hope you looked at 13 ♗xf7+! ♔xf7. With accurate play, White is winning: 14 ♘g5+! (not 14 ♕c4+? ♔e8 15 ♕e6+ ♗e7!) 14...♔e8 (the king is mated if it advances: 14...♔g6 15 ♕e4+! ♔h5 16 g4+ ♔h4 17 ♘f3+ ♔h3 18 ♘g1+ ♔h4 19 ♗g5+! ♔xg5 20 ♕f5+ ♔h4 21 ♕h5# or 14...♔xf6 15 ♕c6+ ♔e5 16 ♕e6+ ♔d4 17 ♕e4+ ♔c3 18 ♗d2#) 15 f7+! (15 ♕e4+? loses to 15...♕e7!! 16 fxe7 bxa1♕ 17 exf8♕++ ♔xf8) 15...♔e7 16 ♕e4+ ♘e5 17 ♕xe5+ ♔d7 18 ♗xb2 and White wins.

Opening Strategy

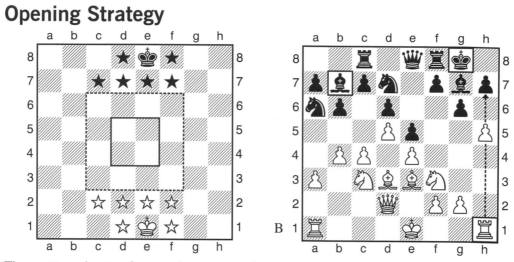

The next two chapters focus on key aspects of opening strategy: development, the centre, and castling – and more generally king safety. The first diagram above clarifies what we mean by the *centre*. The solid box shows the four central squares, while the dotted box is the *extended centre*. The four centre squares are the most important on the board. If you don't control any of these squares, you probably have a very bad position. That's because so many important lines go through these squares, and pieces on a central square radiate power in all directions. Your plans *must* take the centre into account. Note that *control* and *occupy* don't mean the same thing. For instance, a knight on a central square attacks a lot of squares, but doesn't control its own square and needs support from other pieces to avoid being forced away.

We often talk about a 'king in the centre'. In this case we are not saying it is right in the middle of the board (though we saw some examples of that in the previous chapter!). We mean that it isn't safely castled – and generally on one of the marked squares. So should we just castle as soon as we can? Not always. Castling is a big strategic decision, as we'll see in Chapter 8. World Champion Magnus Carlsen made an interesting comment about castling: "I think the general rule for opening play is that if you are one move away from castling you are pretty much always fine. If you are three moves away from castling, you are never fine, and if you are two moves away from castling, it could go either way!" So make sure your king can castle if it needs to, and then make the decision on your own terms.

Development doesn't mean just moving a piece off its starting square. Each piece needs to be doing something purposeful: controlling central squares, supporting threats or working towards a plan. Of course, your first developing moves can't have a specific plan in mind – there are too many possibilities – but as you play more games you'll get a feel for when they are well-placed and when they are not. Sometimes we can develop a piece without even moving it. In the second diagram above, the white rook on h1 is already creating threats on the h-file, whereas Black has moved all his pieces, but none of them are very active: the bishop on b7 would do well to return to c8 to find useful work. On the other hand, White's unmoved rooks could prove useful on either side of the board, and White still has all his castling options.

7 Development and the Centre

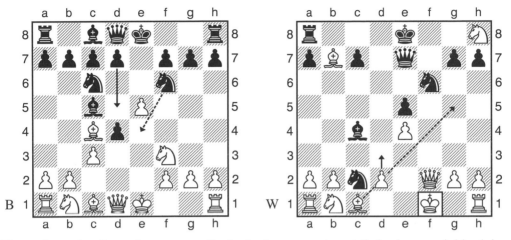

The main goals of opening strategy for both players are to get their pieces quickly doing something useful, and to control the centre of the board. In particular, in the first few moves Black must fight hard to deny White complete domination of the centre, and may need to use tactics to do so. Our first diagram is a typical case where alert play is essential. The moves to consider are 6...d5 and 6...♘e4. 6...♘e4? might be a good idea if Black could secure his knight on this central square by playing ...d5, but 7 ♗d5! rules that out. After 7...f5 (7...♘xf2 8 ♔xf2 dxc3+ 9 ♔g3 doesn't give Black enough for the piece) 8 cxd4 ♗b4+ 9 ♘bd2 (or 9 ♗d2) Black has a new problem: his king will not find a safe home on the kingside. The right move is 6...d5!. After the c4-bishop moves, the black knight will move to e4 and Black will have a share of the centre and good development; e.g., 7 ♗b5 ♘e4 8 cxd4 ♗b6 or 7 ♗e2 ♘e4 8 cxd4 ♗b4+, while 7 exf6?! dxc4 8 fxg7 ♖g8 is good for Black.

Our second position above shows the importance of getting the pieces out quickly. White is well up on material but his development is terrible. 12 d3! simply must be the right move, as it gets White's pieces moving. After 12...♗xd3+ 13 ♔g1 ♘g4 14 ♗c6+ ♔d8 15 ♗g5 we see a specific line where this is valuable – White wins easily here. Instead the greedy 12 ♔g1?? ♘g4 is winning for *Black* because White's queen and king are both in grave danger: 13 ♗c6+ (13 ♗xa8 ♘xf2 14 ♔xf2 ♕f6+ leads to mate) 13...♔d8 14 ♘f7+ and now 14...♔c8! wins since the white queen dare not abandon the g1-a7 diagonal.

- The ...d5 advance is such an important idea for Black that it is worth thinking about in almost any position where White is creating an 'ideal' centre with pawns on d4 and e4.
- A temporary knight sacrifice followed by a pawn fork is a common way to break White's grip on the centre – we shall see several examples in this chapter.
- The player who is in charge of the central squares of the board sets the pace and can quickly move pieces from one part of the board to another.
- If you are behind in development, seek ways to catch up as a matter of urgency.

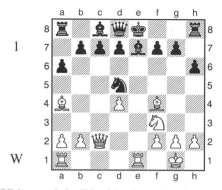

1

White exploits Black's slow development in an amazing way.

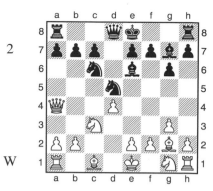

2

Black has developed rapidly, but White's mobile pawns now decide the game.

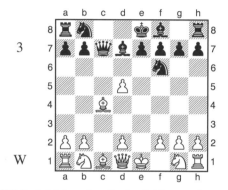

3

White's bishop is attacked. Choose between 7 d3 and 7 ♕b3.

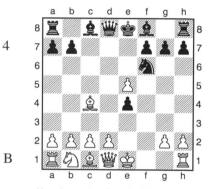

4

Is centralization the key? Choose between 8...♗g4 and 8...♕d4.

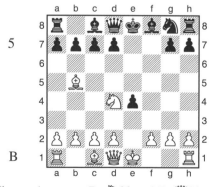

5

Choose between 7...♘f6 and 7...♕f6.

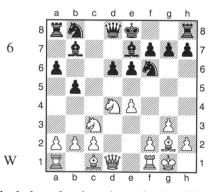

6

Black has developed carelessly. What do you play now?

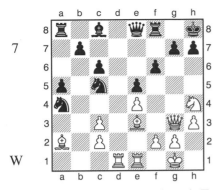

7

W

Black's queenside is undeveloped. Exploit that in dramatic fashion!

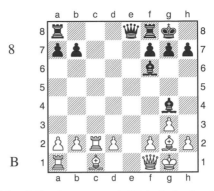

8

B

Take full advantage of White's lack of development.

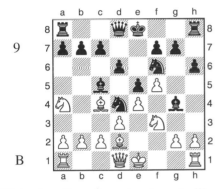

9

B

White has forgotten about controlling the centre. How does Black punish him?

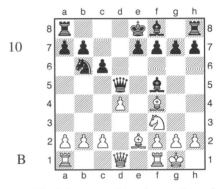

10

B

Does Black have anything better than simply developing?

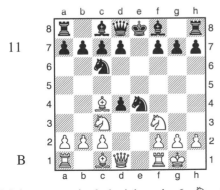

11

B

Make a practical decision: is 6...♘xc3 or 6...dxc3 safer?

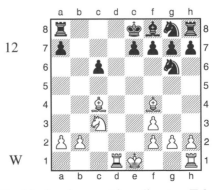

12

W

Black's development is a disaster. Take full advantage and force an immediate win.

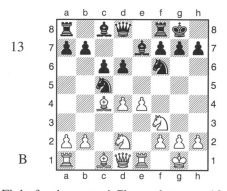

13

B

Fight for the centre! Choose between 10...d5 and 10...♘cxe4.

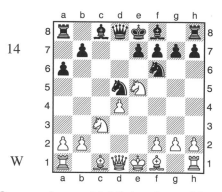

14

W

One good move highlights the problems on Black's queenside.

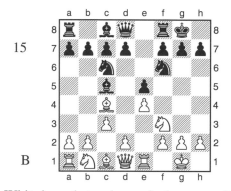

15

B

White is ready to advance in the centre. Stop him in his tracks!

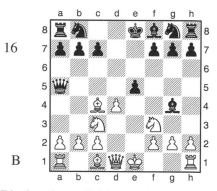

16

B

"Black solves all his problems by playing 6...exd4 7 ♕xd4 ♗xf3." True or false?

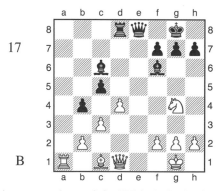

17

B

A neat tactic exploits White's lack of development.

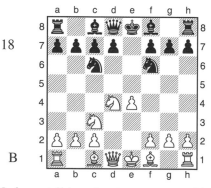

18

B

We keep talking about counterpunching in the centre. So is 5...d5 the right move?

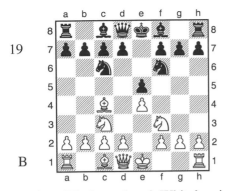

19 B

Show how Black can break White's grip on d5 with a little piece of tactics.

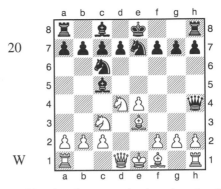

20 W

Black's development looks chaotic. How does White now win a piece?

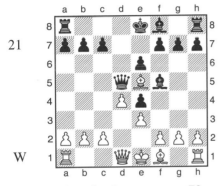

21 W

Should White take the pawn on c7?

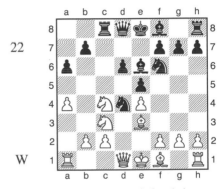

22 W

Is 11 b3 a good way to defend the attacked knight on c4?

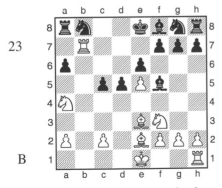

23 B

Should Black continue developing with 12...♞d7 here?

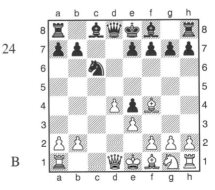

24 B

The position looks quite ordinary, yet Black can force a win. How?

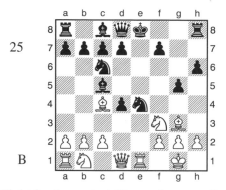

25 B

Fight for the centre! Choose between 9...0-0 and 9...d5.

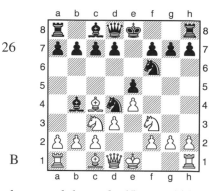

26 B

Is the central thrust 6...d5 a good idea?

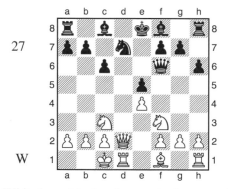

27 W

White has a big development advantage. Put it to use.

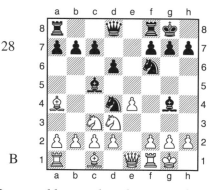

28 B

How would you take advantage of White's slow and awkward development?

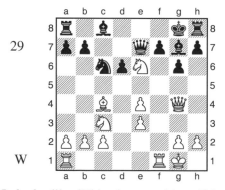

29 W

It looks like White has got himself into a nasty pin, but with one powerful sacrifice he can slice into the black kingside.

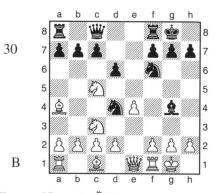

30 B

The sacrifice 10...♞f3+ is a type of idea we have seen before. Does it work here?

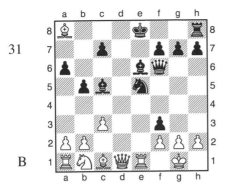

31

Take advantage of White's lack of development and vulnerable king.

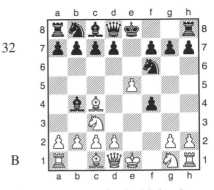

32

Black must get a foothold in the centre. How?

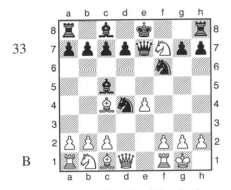

33

It looks desperate for Black but he has a way to stay fully in the game.

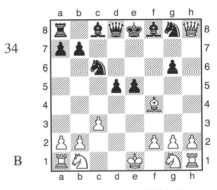

34

What is more important: White's material plus or Black's development?

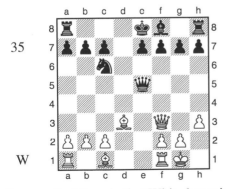

35

Can you find the win that White has missed in several games?

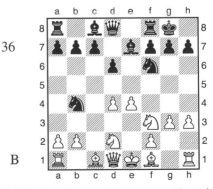

36

White's development is so poor that simple direct play wins for Black.

Solutions to Development and the Centre Exercises

1) 15 ♖xe7+! wins. 15...♕xe7 16 ♖e1 pins the queen, but 15...♘xe7 16 ♗xc7, trapping the queen on its home square, is the main point. After 15...♔xe7 the simplest win is 16 ♕e4+.

2) Black had missed that 8 ♘xd5! paves the way for the pawns to roll forward: 8...♗xd5 9 e4 ♗e6 10 d5 and White wins a piece. Although Black got his pieces out quickly, he failed to establish a central foothold and paid a heavy price. Instead 8 e4?? is bad because of 8...♘b6 followed by taking on d4.

3) If you chose 7 ♕b3??, then you were perhaps thinking too much of your own ideas (i.e. the d6 advance) and not enough about your opponent's possibilities. 7...b5! wins a piece thanks to the pin against the undefended bishop on c1. On the other hand, 7 d3 is a good move that keeps everything solidly defended and prepares further development.

4) 8...♗g4?? hits the queen, but is a blunder because of 9 exf6! ♗xd1 10 ♗b5+, regaining the queen (and keeping an extra piece) because the black king has nowhere to run. Even if you didn't see that, then 9 ♗e2 is also good for White, and reason enough to reject 8...♗g4??. Instead 8...♕d4 is a good move, countering by attacking the c4-bishop and installing the queen on a powerful central square.

5) 7...♘f6?? is a blunder. Even though the pin-based 8 ♘e6! doesn't trap the queen, it wins because 8...♕e7 9 ♘xc7+ picks up the rook on a8. 7...♕f6! is far better, avoiding tactical accidents before catching up with development – the fact that White's pieces aren't well-anchored will help with this.

6) 10 e5! unleashes a *rampant pawn*, creating a double attack on f6 and b7. After 10...♗xg2 11 exf6 Black still has two pieces under attack, so the best he can do is 11...♗xf1 12 fxe7 ♕xe7 13 ♕xf1, though two pieces for rook and pawn is a serious material advantage in the middlegame.

7) The fact that Black's queen's rook is not covering d8 allows White to play 19 ♖d8!, deflecting the queen from its vital role covering the g6-square. After 19...♕xd8 20 ♘g6+! hxg6 21 ♕h4# Black is mated.

8) 17...♗e2! 18 ♕e1 ♗d3! attacks both queen and rook, and after 19 ♕xe8 ♖axe8 White can't save his rook without allowing a deadly check on his back rank: 20 ♖c7 ♖e1+ 21 ♗f1 ♗xf1.

9) By ploughing right through the centre to attack the white king: 9...♘xe4! (9...♘xf3+ 10 gxf3 ♘xe4! is good too) 10 dxe4 (10 ♘xc5 ♗xf3 11 gxf3 ♕h4+ also mates, while 10 h4 ♘g3 is obviously a disaster for White) 10...♘xf3+ 11 gxf3 ♕h4+ leads to mate: 12 ♔e2 ♕f2+ 13 ♔d3 ♕d4+ 14 ♔e2 ♕xe4+ 15 ♔f1 ♗h3#.

10) Yes! The loose bishop on f4 is a clue that there is a double attack in the position: 11...♕e4! wins a pawn on c2.

11) 6...dxc3?! is extremely risky, as White replies 7 ♗xf7+ ♔xf7 8 ♕d5+ ♔f6 (8...♔e8 9 ♖e1) 9 ♖e1 ♘e7 10 ♕xe4 ♔f7 11 ♗g5, when Black may still be better, but in practice anything could happen. 6...♘xc3! is not only safer, but stronger. 7 bxc3 (7 ♖e1+ ♗e7 8 bxc3 is similar) 7...♗e7 8 cxd4 d5 simply leaves Black a pawn up with a great position.

12) With 11 ♘b5! White threatens ♘c7#, and 11...cxb5 allows 12 ♗xb5#, while 11...♖c8 12 ♘c7+ ♖xc7 13 ♗xc7 is hopeless for Black. After 11...e5 12 ♘c7+ ♔e7 13 ♗g5+ f6 14 ♗e3 White threatens ♗c5#, so Black loses a whole rook. 11 ♘d5! is also good, with the same ideas.

13) The answer when Black must fight for the centre in Open Games (i.e. the group of openings starting 1 e4 e5) is often ...d5 or ...♘xe4, so having to choose between them might have proved hard! However, 10...♘cxe4? fails for a tactical reason: after 11 ♘xe4 ♘xe4 12 ♖xe4 the standard pawn fork 12...d5 fails because of 13 ♖xe7, when White gets two pieces for a rook. So 10...d5! is best, meeting 11 e5 (11 dxc5 dxc4) with either 11...♘fe4 or 11...♘fd7.

14) The disruptive check 9 ♕a4+! causes a traffic-jam on the d7-square: 9...♗d7 (9...b5 is no good because of 10 ♗xb5+ as the a6-pawn is pinned against the rook) 10 ♘xd7 and Black has no good reply since 10...♘xd7 drops the d5-knight and 10...♕xd7 11 ♗b5 exploits two pins to win material.

15) The standard pawn-fork trick 6...♘xe4! gives Black an excellent game. 7 d4 (7 ♖xe4?! d5 is even better for Black, who will dominate the centre) 7...exd4 8 cxd4 ♗b4! (not 8...d5?? 9 dxc5 dxc4 10 ♕xd8 ♖xd8 11 ♖xe4) and after both 9 ♗xf7+ ♖xf7 10 ♖xe4 d5 and 9 ♖xe4 d5 10 ♗g5 ♕d7 Black can be completely happy with his development and central control. 6...d5 is possible too, but after 7 exd5 ♘xd5 8 d3, Black has some problems defending his e5-pawn.

16) False. In fact, there is no way for Black to solve his development problems, and 6...exd4 7 ♕xd4 ♗xf3 fails because of 8 ♕e3+! ♗e7 9 ♕xf3 with a decisive double attack on b7 and f7.

17) 21...♗xd4! 22 cxd4 ♖xd4 wins a pawn. 23 ♗d2 (23 ♕f1 ♖xg4 forces a weakening in the white king's pawn-cover) 23...♕d8 24 ♘e3 ♖xd2 25 ♕c1 ♕d4 26 b3 g6 and Black is in full control, threatening further gains with ideas like ...♗xg2.

18) No, it is a bad idea. A counterpunch needs a target, and 5...d5? causes White no inconvenience and only offers up targets to attack. After 6 ♗b5! ♗d7 7 exd5 it is hard for Black to get his pawn back in view of lines like 7...♘xd4 8 ♕xd4 ♗xb5 9 ♘xb5 ♘xd5?? 10 ♕xd5 ♕xd5 11 ♘xc7+. A far better way to strike back in the centre is 5...♗b4 6 ♘xc6 bxc6 7 ♗d3 d5.

19) 4...♘xe4! is best, and the reason why White rarely develops this way. After 5 ♘xe4 the pawn fork 5...d5 wins back the piece and gives Black an excellent game; e.g., 6 ♗d3 dxe4 7 ♗xe4 ♗d6 8 0-0 0-0 9 ♖e1 ♘b4!? intending ...f5. And 5 ♗xf7+?! ♔xf7 6 ♘xe4 d5 is just good for Black, as his king is quite safe while he has good pieces and dominates the centre.

20) The piece-win is only two moves deep, but several players have missed it over the board. First 7 ♘f3! creates a double attack, which 7...♕h5 parries. However, the queen can then be deflected by 8 g4!, and after the queen saves its skin, 9 ♗xc5 bags a free piece.

21) No, 10 ♗xc7? is a terrible pawn-grab. It wastes time when White is behind in development and opens critical lines for the black pieces. After 10...♖c8 White must already hit the emergency button with 11 g4, but after 11...♖xc7 12 gxf5 ♕a5+ 13 c3 ♖xc3! 14 bxc3 ♕xc3+ he will be struggling to survive. Bishop retreats lose: 11 ♗e5? ♕a5+! 12 c3 (also hopeless are 12 ♕d2 ♗b4 and 12 ♔e2 ♕b5+ followed by ...♕xb2) 12...♖xc3! 13 ♕d2 (13 bxc3 ♕xc3+ picks off the rook since 14 ♔e2? ♕c4+ 15 ♔e1 ♗b4+ is the end) 13...♗b4! and White is busted; e.g., 14 a3 ♖c1+ or 14 ♔e2 ♖c6.

22) 11 b3? is bad because Black opens lines with the central break 11...d5!, with the specific aim of pinning the knight on c3 that White has just left unprotected. Then 12 ♘xd5 ♘xe4 strands the knight on d5, while 12 ♘xe5 has numerous good answers, including 12...♗b4! 13 ♗xd4 ♖xc3!. And 12 exd5 ♗b4 leaves White in deep trouble: 13 dxe6 ♗xc3+ 14 ♗d2 ♗xa1 or 13 ♗d2 ♗g4 14 f3 (14 ♕c1 ♗f5) 14...♗xf3! 15 gxf3 ♘xd5!.

23) Yes, 12...♘d7! is Black's best move. White has a fork trick with 13 ♖xd7? ♔xd7 14 ♘b6+ but after 14...♔c6 15 ♘xa8 ♘h6 the knight is trapped and Black is doing well.

24) 8...e5! opens lines and activates pieces without loss of time. With the white king so exposed to diagonal attack, this is enough to win! 9 ♗xe5 (9 dxe5 ♕a5+! is no different) 9...♕a5+! (9...♗b4+ 10 ♔e2 allows White to limp on a little longer) 10 ♔e2 (or 10 ♕d2 ♗b4) 10...♕b5+ 11 ♔d2 (after 11 ♔e1 ♗b4+ the white queen is lost) 11...♕xb2+ and White loses a rook, with more to follow.

25) 9...0-0! makes use of the pawn fork 10 ♖xe4 d5 to give Black a big advantage. This is far better than 9...d5?, when 10 ♗xd5! ♕xd5 11 ♘c3 is a standard tactic that offers White good play.

26) Yes, 6...d5! is an excellent move, activating Black's pieces and giving White serious problems. After 7 exd5 it is important that Black replies 7...♗g4! with a strong pin on the white knight and keeping the almighty black knight on d4. Regaining the pawn on d5 can wait until later. White's king will lack good pawn-cover and he faces a tough fight to survive. 7 ♗xd5 ♘xd5 8 exd5 ♗g4! is similar.

27) White must act now, as otherwise Black will develop and have an excellent game. 10 ♘b5! cxb5 (10...♖b8 11 ♘xa7 and 10...♔d8 11 ♕c3 cxb5 12 ♗xb5 ♗d6 13 ♖d3, intending ♖hd1, are also terrible for Black) 11 ♗xb5 and Black has no good defence since after 11...♕e6 12 ♘xe5! White will win back the piece on d7 because 12...♕xe5 13 ♗xd7+ is destructive.

28) 9...♘f3+!! gives Black a winning attack. After 10 gxf3 ♗xf3 Black threatens to bring his queen in with ...♕c8-h3 or ...♘h5 and ...♕g5, and White will have to give up his queen just to avoid a quick mate. 11 ♘f4 (11 ♘xc5 ♘g4 intending ...♕h4; 11 h3 forces Black to find the accurate 11...♘g4!, preventing ♔h2 while threatening ...♕h4; e.g., 12 ♘e2 ♕h4 13 ♘df4 g5) 11...♘d5!? 12 ♘fe2 (12 ♘h5 ♘f4!? 13 ♘xf4 ♕g5+) and now the cleanest win is 12...♘f4! 13 h3 ♕g5+ 14 ♘g3 ♕xg3#.

29) 14 ♖xf7!! brilliantly exploits Black's chaotic kingside development. Then 14...♕xf7 15 ♖f1 ♗f6 (15...♕e7 16 ♘c7+! leads to mate) 16 ♘d5 ♗e6 17 ♘xf6+ is hopeless for Black, while after 14...♔xf7 15 ♘c7+ ♔f8 (15...d5 has several good answers, including 16 ♗xd5+ ♔f8 17 ♕f4+ and ♘xa8) 16 ♖f1+ ♗f6 17 ♕f4 ♔g7 18 ♘3d5 White wins back material and keeps a strong grip on the position.

30) No, 10...♘f3+? (10...♗f3 is better) 11 gxf3 ♗xf3 fails here because 12 ♘d7! blocks the queen long enough for White to give his king some squares: 12...♘xd7 13 ♕e3 ♘e5 14 ♕f4 f5 15 d4! fxe4 (15...♖f6 16 exf5) 16 ♕g3 and Black's attack is not breaking through.

31) 13...♗xf2+! 14 ♔xf2 (14 ♔h1 ♗xe1 is simply good for Black since 15 ♕xe1? loses to 15...f2 16 ♕f1 ♗c4) 14...♕h4+! (not 14...♘g4+? 15 ♔g3!) 15 ♔e3 (no better are 15 ♔f1 ♗c4+ 16 ♔g1 f2+ and 15 g3 ♕xh2+ 16 ♔e3 f2) 15...fxg2 16 ♗xg2 0-0 with a decisive attack on the white king, which cannot be saved despite White's huge material advantage; e.g., 17 ♘d2 ♘g4+ 18 ♔d3 ♘f2+ 19 ♔c2 ♗f5+ 20 ♗e4 ♘xd1 21 ♔xd1 ♖e8.

32) 5...d5! is the only good move here, counterattacking the white bishop and getting a share of the centre. 6 exf6 dxc4 poses no danger for Black after 7 fxg7 ♖g8 or 7 ♕e2+ ♗e6. The same can be said of 6 ♗b3 ♘e4!, while 6 ♗b5+ ♘fd7 7 ♘xd5 ♗a5! is also comfortable for Black. Other moves in the diagram position are bad. If Black meekly retreats his knight then he is simply getting pushed around, while 5...♕e7? 6 ♕e2 certainly doesn't help. 5...♗xc3? 6 dxc3! is also bad for Black: 6...d5 (or 6...♘e4 7 ♗xf4 with central domination) 7 exf6 dxc4 8 ♕xd8+ will leave White a pawn up.

33) Black needs to strike in the centre right away and make the most of his active pieces: 7...d5! 8 ♘xh8? (too greedy; White needs to think of his own survival: 8 c3 ♗g4 9 ♕a4+ ♗d7 10 ♕d1 stays afloat, when 10...♗g4 repeats the position) 8...♗g4! 9 ♕d2 (9 f3? loses to 9...♘xf3++ 10 ♔h1 ♘xh2) 9...dxc4 10 ♘c3 (10 ♕g5 0-0-0 11 e5 ♗e6 12 exf6 gxf6 followed by ...♘xc2 leaves Black in charge) 10...0-0-0 11 ♕g5 and now 11...h6! (not 11...♖xh8? 12 e5) 12 ♕f4 g5! keeps a material plus.

34) As long as he plays 10...exf4! 11 ♕xg8 ♗f5 Black has a decisive attack thanks to his active pieces and White's exposed king. ...♕e7+ and ...0-0-0 are coming, and White's lone queen provides no real counterplay. One game ended 12 ♕h7 ♘e5 13 ♕xb7 ♖b8 14 ♕xa7 ♗c5!? 15 ♕g7 ♘d3+ 16 ♔e2 ♕h4 17 ♘h3 ♕g4+, mating.

35) 11 ♗a6! wins. The first game where this was missed featured future world champion Karpov as Black. 11...e6 (or: 11...bxa6? 12 ♕xc6+ ♔d8 13 ♕xa8+; 11...0-0-0 12 ♕xc6 bxa6 13 ♕xa6+ ♔b8 14 ♗e3; 11...♕d6 12 ♗xb7 ♘d4 13 ♕e3 ♖b8 14 ♗e4 and Black will be slaughtered on the centre files) 12 ♗f4! (12 ♗xb7 ♘d4 is less clear) and Black is busted; e.g., 12...♗c5 13 ♗xb7 ♘d4 14 ♕e4 or 12...♕xb2 13 ♖ab1 ♘d4 14 ♕e4 ♕xc2 15 ♕xb7.

36) Unfortunately, 10...♘xe4? doesn't quite work: 11 ♘xe4 ♗f5 (11...d5 12 ♘c5) 12 ♗d2 (or 12 a3) 12...d5 13 ♗xb4 dxe4 14 ♗e7. But 10...d5! simply slices through the centre: 11 e5 (after 11 a3 dxe4 12 axb4 exf3 White is material down and his king is in deep trouble) 11...♗f5 and there is no way to defend the c2-square. 12 exf6 ♘c2+ 13 ♔e2 ♕e8!? is a disaster for White's king, while 12 ♗b5 ♘c2+ 13 ♔f1 ♘xa1 14 exf6 ♗xf6 15 ♗a4 c6 intends ...b5, rescuing the knight.

ATTACK THE CENTRE

8 Castling

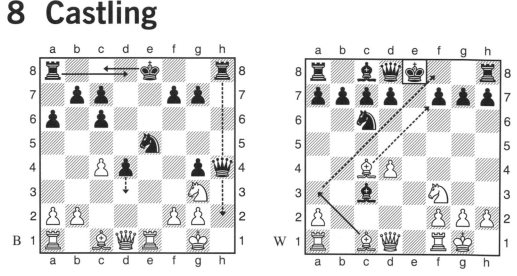

"Get safely castled!" We've all heard this advice, particularly after games where we didn't! Securing the king is one of the key goals of opening strategy, and castling is the standard way to do so. But there is far more to castling than that. By choosing where our king will live, we define our plans for the middlegame, but clarify our opponent's options too. In this short chapter, we look at the consequences of failing to castle, and various ways to prevent the opponent from castling. We also see castling as a tactical resource – it sometimes wins on the spot! – and take a look at cases where it loses instantly to a nasty tactic (more on that in the next chapter).

In our first diagram, 16...0-0-0! is a multi-purpose move that wins the game. It unpins the knight and supports the d-pawn. After 17 ♖xe5 d3! the pawn covers the e2-square, so Black is threatening 18...♕h2+ 19 ♔f1 ♕h1+! 20 ♘xh1 ♖xh1#, to which White has no good reply. Even after 18 ♖h5 ♖xh5 19 ♘xh5 ♕xh5 20 ♗f4 ♖h8 White can't avoid mate.

In the second position, White has a big lead in development, and must choose the best way to put it to use. 10 ♖b1? d5! (remember this move from the previous chapter?) is an example of the wrong approach, while 10 ♕b3 d5 11 ♗xd5 0-0 and 10 ♗xf7+ ♔xf7 11 ♘g5+ ♔g8 are both good for White, but give Black chances of surviving. The main point is that you have to be aggressive, and stopping Black from castling, even at a heavy material cost, is the best path: 10 ♗a3! d5 11 ♗b5! ♗xa1 12 ♖e1+ ♗e6 and now 13 ♕xa1?! is not aggressive enough, but 13 ♕c2! leaves Black defenceless, as 13...♕d7 runs into 14 ♘e5 – Black is pinned to death.

- Castling is both a king move *and* a rook move! Think about where you want your *rooks* to be for the middlegame.
- Occasionally, castling can create a double attack when an enemy rook or knight has wandered too close.
- Before castling, check that you aren't castling directly into a winning attack.
- If you are two moves away from castling, the opponent has rapid development and the centre is open, this is already an emergency! Get your king to safety!

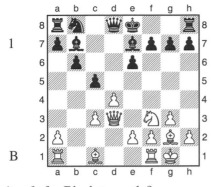

1

Is it safe for Black to castle?

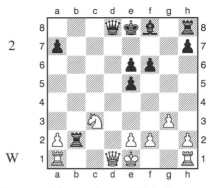

2

What would you play as White?

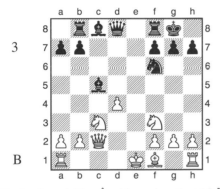

3

Black played 11...♗xd4, seeing that 12 ♖d1 ♗xc3+ is no problem. What had he missed?

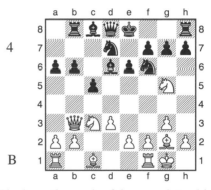

4

"Black castles and safely completes his development." True or false?

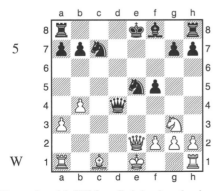

5

How should White finish developing: 17 ♗b2 or 17 0-0?

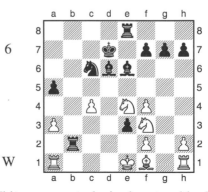

6

White appears to be in deep trouble. How does he escape?

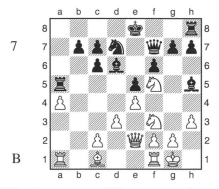

White has prevented his opponent from castling. Why? After 16...0-0? what happens?

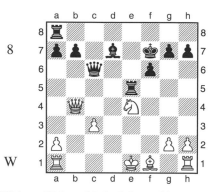

"White will lose his knight and have to fight for a draw." True or false?

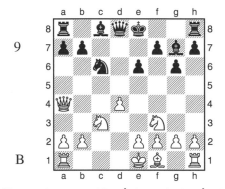

Choose between 10...♗d7 and 10...♗xd4.

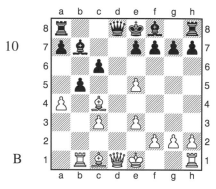

"White has cleverly exploited a pin on the b-file." True or false?

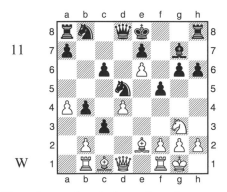

How do you break through to the uncastled black king?

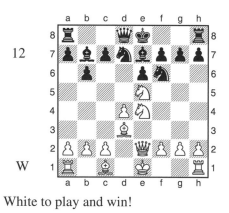

White to play and win!

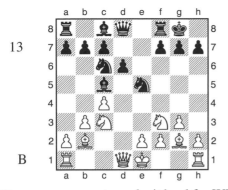

13

Do you see a way to make it hard for White to complete his development?

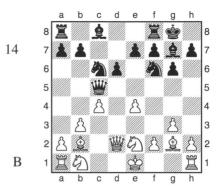

14

White is about to castle and finish developing. How do you stop that?

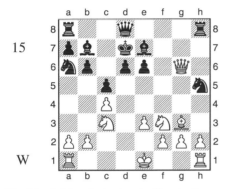

15

The black king is trying to flee to the queenside. Why won't that work?

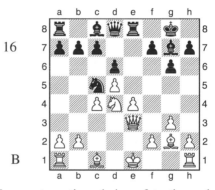

16

From a tempting choice of tactics, what is Black's best option?

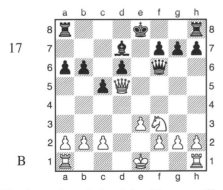

17

Black needs to defend the d6-pawn. Choose between 13...♚e7 and 13...0-0-0.

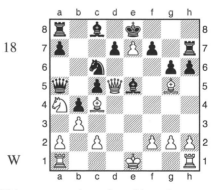

18

White apparently resigned here in one game. Is it worth playing on?

Solutions to Castling Exercises

1) No, 10...0-0?? would be a terrible mistake as it allows a standard opening tactic: 11 Ng5! is a double attack against b7 and h7, and after 11...Bxg5 (11...Bxg2 12 Qxh7#) 12 Bxb7 Black loses rook for bishop.

2) 14 Qxd8+! Kxd8 15 0-0-0+! wins a rook.

3) 11...Bxd4?? loses because 12 0-0-0! also pins the bishop while ruling out the saving reply ...Bxc3+. So Black simply loses his bishop.

4) False! 11...0-0?? allows 12 Nxe6! with a catastrophic material loss for Black because 12...fxe6 13 Qxe6+ forks king and d6-bishop. Instead 11...Bc7 or even 11...h6 is safe.

5) 17 Bb2?? is a fatal blunder because of the fork 17...Qxb2! 18 Qxb2 Nd3+. With 17 0-0! White intends Bb2, winning back the knight with an excellent game. Even if you weren't able to assess the complications after 17...Qxa1 18 Bf4! Qxa3 (or 18...Qd4 19 Bxe5) 19 Qxe5+ (White is doing very well indeed!), it is clear that this is better than falling for the fork trick.

6) 19 0-0-0! creates a sudden double attack on the b2-rook and d6-bishop. After 19...Reb8? 20 Rxd6+ Kc7 21 fxe3! White is a piece up. Black's only hope is 19...Rd2 20 Nfxd2 Bxa3+ 21 Kc2 exd2, though White has all the chances here.

7) 16...0-0? runs into 17 Bh6! followed by taking on g7 since 17...gxh6? 18 Nxh6+ is a deadly knight fork.

8) False. 20 0-0-0! unpins the knight and counterattacks the black bishop. 20...Rxe4 (otherwise Black is just a piece down) 21 Rxd7+! leaves the queen overloaded, and 21...Ke8 is neatly met by 22 Re7+! Rxe7 23 Bb5, winning the black queen.

9) 10...Bd7! gives Black very active play; e.g., 11 Qd1 Qb6. Even if you were unsure if Black was OK there, you could have rejected the other option if you saw that 10...Bxd4?? loses a piece after 11 0-0-0!, because of the deadly pin on the d-file. 11...e5 is answered with 12 e3.

10) False, because after 11...Qxd1+! 12 Kxd1 Black wins with either 12...bxc4 13 Rxb7 0-0-0+! or the simpler 12...0-0-0+! followed by ...bxc4.

11) 17 Nxf5? gxf5 18 Bh5+ Kf8 is unclear since White has already burnt a good attacking piece without getting his queen into the action. 17 Bh5! is best. Then 17...gxh5? allows 18 Qxh5+ Kf8 19 Qf7#, while otherwise White wins the pawns on g6 and f5 and gets the black king on the run.

12) White must strike before Black castles, and 9 Nxf7! fits the bill perfectly: 9...Kxf7 10 Ng5+ Ke8 11 Nxe6 Qc8 (11...Bb4+ 12 c3 Qe7 13 cxb4 is clearly hopeless for Black, as he is already material down) 12 Nxg7+ Kf7 (12...Kd8 13 Bh6 intending 0-0-0 and Rhe1) 13 Qe6+ Kxg7 14 Qxe7+ Kg8 15 Bc4+ and White mates: 15...Bd5 16 Bxd5+ Nxd5 17 Qe6+ Kg7 18 Bh6#.

13) Yes, we can prevent White from castling by playing 9...Nxf3+! 10 Bxf3 (or 10 exf3 Re8+, when White must play 11 Kf1 because 11 Ne2? Qe7 is a nasty pin) 10...Bh3. While Black may not be much better objectively, White suddenly has some problems to solve. For instance, 11 Nd5 (intending a3 followed by Nf4) 11...Ne5 12 Be4? c6 puts White in deep trouble because 13 Nf4 loses to 13...Bb4+ and 13 Nc3 Ng4 14 e3 Qg5 leaves Black with a huge attack.

14) 10...♗h3!! brilliantly ruins White's plans by exploiting the overloaded bishop on g2. Then 11 ♗xh3? ♘xe4 hits b2, d2 and f2, winning on the spot. 11 b4? ♘xb4 doesn't help White at all, and 11 0-0 ♗xg2 12 ♔xg2 ♘xe4 costs White a vital pawn. 11 ♗f3 is clearly very bad for White's development, which is already a big success for Black. If you also saw that 11...♘e5 12 ♗xe5 dxe5 intends ...♖ad8 with further pain for White, well done.

15) 14 ♘e5+! either opens the d-file or brings extra pieces into the attack. The king may make it to the queenside, but it will die there. After 14...dxe5 (declining is no better: 14...♔c7 15 ♘b5+ ♔b8 16 ♘f7 and 14...♔c8 15 ♕xe6+ ♔b8 16 ♘d7+ both cost Black material without ending the attack) 15 0-0-0+! (15 ♖d1+? ♗d6 16 ♗xe5 ♕g8 gives Black more survival chances) 15...♗d5 (15...♗d6 is now met by 16 ♖xd6+ ♔xd6 17 ♖d1+) 16 cxd5 the d-file and the two diagonals leading to Black's queenside will be opened. There's no defence; e.g., 16...♕g8 17 dxe6++ ♔c8 18 ♕e4 ♘c7 19 ♖d7 ♕xe6 20 ♖xc7+ ♔xc7 21 ♘b5+, etc.

16) 13...♗h3! (13...♘xe4? 14 ♗xe4 is much less clear, while 13...♕f6 14 ♘e2 is also not obviously winning for Black) has the point 14 ♗xh3 ♖xe4 (14...♗xd4 followed by ...♖xe4+ is also very strong) 15 0-0 ♖xe3 16 ♗xe3 and Black should win. Instead 14 ♗f3 leaves the white king stranded in the centre. Then Black has many good paths, including 14...c6 intending ...♕b6, but not 14...♘xe4?! 15 ♗xe4 ♗g2?! 16 ♘e6!.

17) 13...♔c7?! 14 0-0-0 condemns Black to a grim defence of his weaknesses. 13...0-0-0! looks crazy, but is more ambitious and works well. Black intends to solve the problem of his backward d-pawn with ...♔c7 and ....♗c6, and the obvious reply 14 ♕a8+?! ♔c7 15 ♕a7+ (15 ♕xa6 ♕xb2 is similar) 15...♔c6! 16 ♕xa6 ♕xb2 17 0-0 ♖a8 only spells trouble for White, while 14 0-0-0 ♔c7 15 ♘g5 ♕e7!? is OK for Black.

18) Yes, absolutely! White's pieces dominate the board, and he can bring both rooks into play with 15 0-0-0! hxg5 16 h4!, when Black's extra piece will be little comfort to him. If you saw this far and felt that White had at least interesting play, then consider the exercise solved. The following lines show White is winning: 16...gxh4? 17 ♖xh4; 16...♕c7 17 hxg5 ♘xe7 18 ♕xa8; 16...♔xe7 17 ♖de1 f6 18 ♕g8; 16...g4 17 h5! g5 18 ♗d3! ♖h6 19 ♗g6! fxg6 20 ♖he1!.

GENERAL TACTICS

9 Does ♗xh7+ Work?

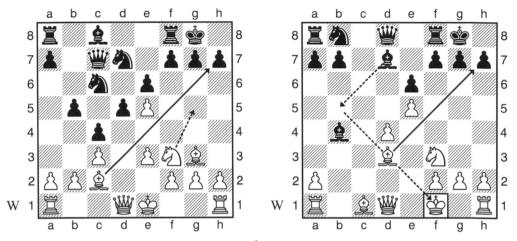

A whole chapter about one move? Yes, but ♗xh7+ is the most common sacrifice against a king that has just castled, so it's a major opening theme too. The sacrifice can have several purposes, including a double attack, but the most common idea (the 'Greek Gift') is to launch a mating attack by ripping open the king and quickly bringing in a knight and queen.

Our first diagram shows a typical example. There is no black piece covering g5, and 13 ♗xh7+! ♔xh7 14 ♘g5+ wins. Black has three king moves, and each must be examined. 14...♔g8?! 15 ♕h5 leads to a standard 'Greco' mate: 15...♖d8 16 ♕xf7+! ♔h8 17 ♕h5+ ♔g8 18 ♕h7+ ♔f8 19 ♕h8+ ♔e7 20 ♕xg7+ ♔e8 21 ♕f7#, while 14...♔g6?! loses to 15 ♕c2+ f5 (15...♔xg5 16 ♗f4+ ♔h5 17 ♕h7+ ♔g4 18 f3#) 16 exf6+ ♔xg5 17 ♗xc7. The most stubborn defence here is 14...♔h6!?, but 15 ♗f4! ♔g6 16 ♕c2+ f5 17 exf6+ wins.

In general there are four ways for Black to respond:

- Decline with ...♔h8. Normally this leaves Black a pawn down with an exposed king, but it may be good if Black has strong threats of his own and just needs to avoid being mated!
- After ♘g5+, put the king on g8. This is good if Black can bring in a piece to defend h7 or if the king can safely run to the queenside.
- After ♘g5+, put the king on h6. It can work well if White has no dark-squared bishop.
- After ♘g5+, put the king on g6. This is often the critical test. It all depends on what queen checks White has, or if he can add extra pieces to the attack, such as bringing the other knight to f4 or a pawn to h5.

I'd like you to come away from this chapter with an ability to assess if the ♗xh7+ sacrifice either fails completely, or if it wins on the spot. The most common case of total failure comes if Black can cover h7, as seen in our second example above. Here 12 ♗xh7+?? is bad because Black defends along the b1-h7 diagonal thanks to a tempo-gain on the white king: 12...♔xh7! 13 ♘g5+ ♔g8! 14 ♕h5 ♗b5+ 15 ♔g1 ♗d3. If White's king had been better placed (e.g. castled), then his sacrifice would have won.

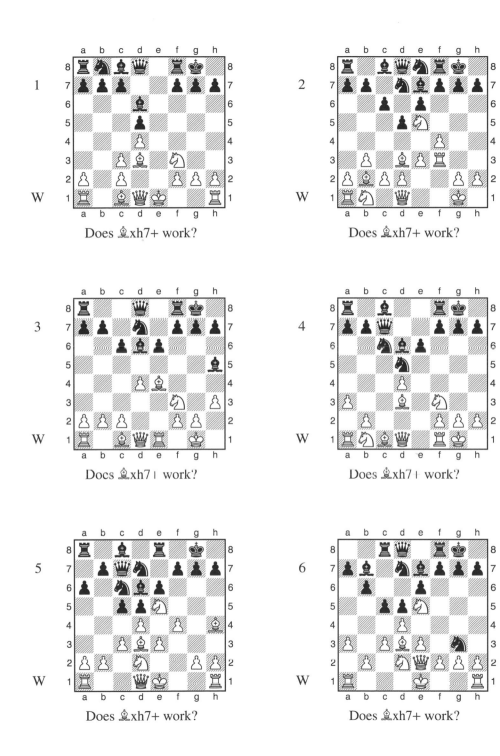

1 Does ♗xh7+ work?

2 Does ♗xh7+ work?

3 Does ♗xh7+ work?

4 Does ♗xh7+ work?

5 Does ♗xh7+ work?

6 Does ♗xh7+ work?

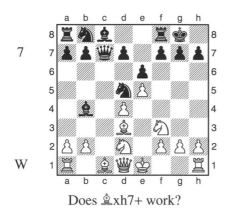

7

Does ♗xh7+ work?

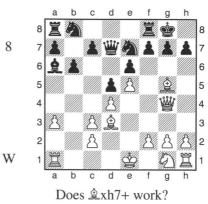

8

Does ♗xh7+ work?

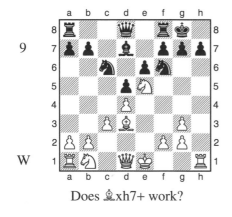

9

Does ♗xh7+ work?

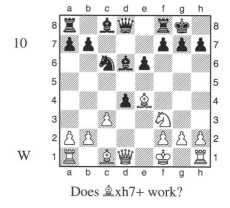

10

Does ♗xh7+ work?

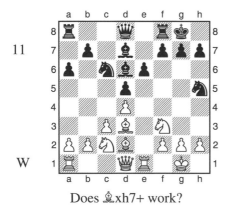

11

Does ♗xh7+ work?

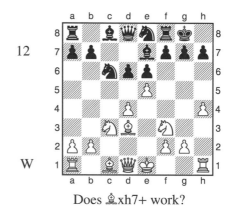

12

Does ♗xh7+ work?

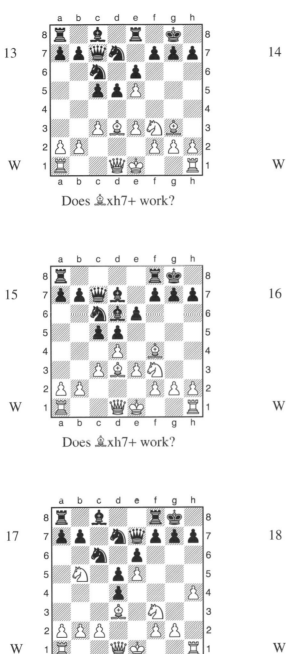

13

W

Does ♗xh7+ work?

14

W

Does ♗xh7+ work?

15

W

Does ♗xh7+ work?

16

W

Docs ♗xh7+ work?

17

W

Does ♗xh7+ work?

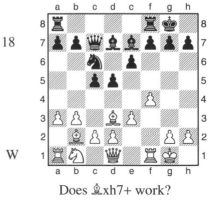

18

W

Does ♗xh7+ work?

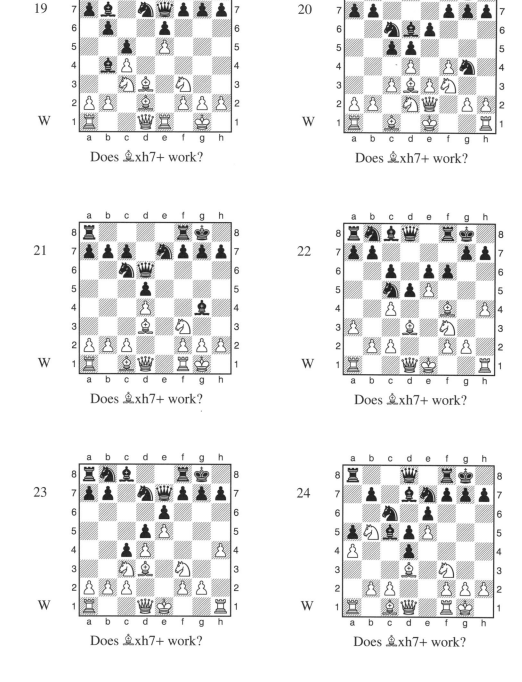

19 W

Does ♗xh7+ work?

20 W

Does ♗xh7+ work?

21 W

Does ♗xh7+ work?

22 W

Does ♗xh7+ work?

23 W

Does ♗xh7+ work?

24 W

Does ♗xh7+ work?

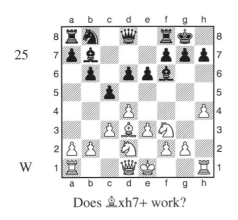

25

Does ♗xh7+ work?

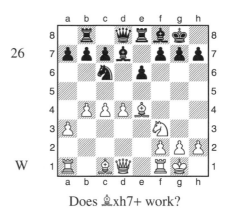

26

Does ♗xh7+ work?

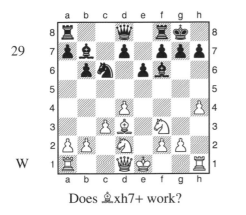

27

Does ♗xh7+ work?

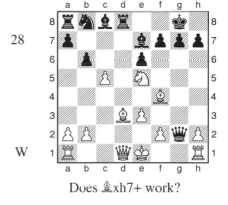

28

Does ♗xh7+ work?

29

Does ♗xh7+ work?

30

Does ♗xh7+ work?

Solutions to 'Does &xh7+ Work?' Exercises

1) No, 9 &xh7+?? is bad because after 9...&xh7 10 ♘g5+ &g8! 11 ♕h5 Black covers h7 with 11...&f5 and is simply a piece up.

2) Yes, 11 &xh7+! wins rather easily. After 11...&xh7 12 ♖h3+ &g8 13 ♕h5 Black has no good defence against the threat of mate on h8.

3) 12 &xh7+?? falls at the first hurdle because 12...&xh7 13 ♘g5+ is taken by the queen: 13...♕xg5 and Black wins because the white queen is also *en prise*.

4) 11 &xh7+?? is no good because Black can defend the h7-square with 11...&xh7 12 ♘g5+ &g8 13 ♕h5 ♘f6. That's why in a successful Greek Gift White often has a pawn on e5.

5) 12 &xh7+! wins because White crashes through on f7 and picks off the e8-rook: 12...&xh7 13 ♕h5+ &g8 14 ♕xf7+ &h7 15 ♕xe8.

6) 13 &xh7+! wins because with his last move, Black gifted White an open h-file: 13...&xh7 14 hxg3+ &g8 15 ♕h5. Be careful exchanging pieces on g3 when the rook is still on h1!

7) 9 &xh7+?? fails because Black's queen has access to the b1-h7 diagonal. After 9...&xh7 10 ♘g5+ &g8! 11 ♕h5 ♕c2! the h7-square is defended and ...♕g6 will end the attack.

8) 10 &xh7+! is good, and based on a fork that wins a pawn: 10...&xh7 11 ♕h4+ &g8 12 &xe7. But that's not all, since White has a winning attack based on the idea of mating with queen and bishop on g7; e.g., 12...♕b5 13 0-0-0 ♘d7 14 &f6 (threatening ♕g5) 14...gxf6 15 ♕g4+ &h7 16 ♖d3.

9) An open h-file is a big help, and 11 &xh7+! indeed wins. After 11...♘xh7 12 ♕h5 Black can't even delay mate for very long: 12...♖e8 13 ♕xf7+ &h8 14 ♘g6#.

10) 11 &xh7+? fails because White doesn't have enough active pieces to mate the king if it walks out into the open: 11...&xh7 12 ♘g5+ &g6! (not 12...&g8?? 13 ♕h5 ♖e8 with the standard Greco mate: 14 ♕xf7+ &h8 15 ♕h5+ &g8 16 ♕h7+ &f8 17 ♕h8+ &e7 18 ♕xg7#) and it's all looking a bit hopeless: 13 ♕g4 f5 or 13 h4 &f6, while with no pawn on e5, 13 ♕d3+ even gives Black a choice between 13...&f6 and 13...f5 – either way White has nothing.

11) 13 &xh7+? is bad because White lacks a good follow-up after 13...&xh7 14 ♘g5+ &g6!. There's no check on the b1-h7 diagonal, and 15 ♕g4 f5 gets White nowhere because g3 is not available to the queen.

12) 10 &xh7+! wins because after 10...&xh7 11 ♘g5+ taking the knight opens the h-file with disastrous consequences for the black king (11...&xg5 12 hxg5+ &g6 13 ♕h5+ &f5 14 g4#), while 11...&g6 12 ♕d3+ is also fatal; e.g., 12...f5 13 exf6+ &xf6 14 ♘ce4+ &g6 15 h5+ &h6 16 ♘f7++ &h7 17 ♘f6#.

13) 12 &xh7+? is no good because after 12...&xh7 13 ♘g5+ &g8, Black can cover h7: 14 ♕h5 ♘f8. There's a saying that you can't get mated with a knight on f8. It's not always true, but here White can't even make any real threats. And after 14 ♘xf7 there are various good answers, including 14...♖f8!, when White has lost the initiative.

14) No. 14 &xh7+? &xh7 15 ♕h5+ &g8 16 ♘g5 would win for White if his king were safe, but as it is Black can play 16...♕xe5+ 17 &f1 ♕f5, bringing his queen into the defence.

15) No, because after 11 &xh7+? &xh7 12 ♘g5+ &g6! White has no good follow-up, as he would if his pawn were on e5 instead of e3. 13 ♕d3+? f5 gives White nothing, while after 13 ♕g4 f5! 14 ♕g3 &xf4 15 exf4 &f6 the king successfully flees to safety.

16) 12 ♗xh7+! ♔xh7 13 ♘g5+ wins here, even though the black queen can come to c2 after 13...♔g8 (advancing with 13...♔g6 14 ♕g4 f5 15 ♕h4 leads to mate) 14 ♕h5 ♕xc2. That's because the queen was overworked, also needing to guard the b4-knight, which 15 ♗xb4 now picks off.

17) 11 ♗xh7+? is no good because White has nothing against the ...♔h6 defence: 11...♔xh7! 12 ♘g5+ ♔h6! and with only one diagonal-moving piece left (i.e. his queen), White can't control enough squares to create real threats: 13 ♕d3 (13 ♕d2 doesn't threaten much and falls foul of 13...♕b4 in any case) 13...f5 14 exf6 gxf6 and White has nothing as long as Black doesn't unwisely take on g5 next move. So when White has no dark-squared bishop, spare a thought for the ...♔h6 defence.

18) Yes, 11 ♗xh7+! is the start of a successful *double bishop sacrifice*: 11...♔xh7 12 ♕h5+ ♔g8 13 ♗xg7! and after 13...♔xg7 14 ♕g4+ ♔h8 the rook-lift 15 ♖f3!, intending ♖h3+, adds the finishing touch. And following 13...f5 14 ♖f3! (not 14 ♕g6? ♗e8) Black will have to shed material to stave off the mating ideas: 14...♗f6 (14...♔xg7 15 ♖g3+ ♔g5 16 ♖xg5+ ♔f6 17 ♕h7!) 15 ♗xf6 ♖xf6 16 ♖g3+ ♔f8 17 ♕h7.

19) 13 ♗xh7+?! is only equal, so is a poor choice given that the diagram position is good for White if he plays normal moves (e.g., 13 ♘g5 g6 14 ♕g4 with heavy kingside pressure). After 13...♔xh7 14 ♘g5+ ♔g8! 15 ♕h5, 15...♘ef6! gives back the piece to kill White's mating ideas. After 16 ♕h4 ♘xe5 17 ♖xe5 ♕d7, intending ...♕d4, or 16 exf6 ♘xf6 17 ♕h4 ♖fd8 Black is OK: 18 ♗f4 ♖d4 19 ♖e3 ♕d8 20 ♖h3 ♔f8, etc.

20) 9 ♗xh7+?! is at best unclear (whereas 9 ♘e5 gives White good play). After 9...♔xh7 10 ♘g5+ ♔g8 11 ♕xg4 it looks like White has won a pawn, but Black gets superb counterplay in the centre with 11...f6 12 ♘xe6 (12 ♘gf3 e5 and White is getting pushed around) 12...♕e7 13 f5 ♗xe6 14 fxe6 f5. White burnt up his active pieces, leaving only passive ones once the black king was safe.

21) Not really. White should play a normal move like 10 c3 with a pleasant game due to the bishop-pair. After 10 ♗xh7+?! Black must reply 10...♔h8! (since 10...♔xh7?? 11 ♘g5+ costs him the bishop), when after 11 ♗d3 ♘xd4 Black wins back the pawn with some advantage since White's kingside will be weakened. Never forget that the ...♔h8 option exists!

22) Even though Black is protecting the g5-square, 11 ♗xh7+! wins because after 11...♔xh7 12 ♘g5+, 12...fxg5 (12...♔g8 13 ♕h5 fxg5 14 hxg5 is the same) 13 hxg5+ fatally opens the h-file: 13...♔g8 (13...♔g6 14 ♕h5+ ♔f5 15 g6+ ♔xf4 16 g3+ ♔e4 17 0-0-0 mates) 14 ♕h5 and Black is mated or loses his queen. 12...♔g6 also loses: 13 h5+ ♔f5 (13...♔h6 14 ♘f7+) 14 ♕f3 fxe5 15 ♗e3#.

23) 10 ♗xh7+! is strong, but after 10...♔xh7 11 ♘g5+ I hoped you looked at 11...♔h6 (rather than 11...♔g8?? 12 ♕h5 or 11...♔g6? 12 ♘e2), which is the key defence. White has a strong attack, and can emerge ahead on material: 12 ♕d2 (12 ♘e2!? is also good) 12...f6 13 ♘xe6+ ♔h7 14 ♘xf8+ and ♘xd5.

24) Sort of. It leads to sharp but balanced play, but White has no obviously better options, so it could be considered a good practical try. 11 ♗xh7+!? ♔xh7 12 ♘g5+ ♔g6! (only move) 13 ♖e1 (better than 13 ♕d3+?! ♘f5! 14 g4 f6) 13...f6 (13...♘f5 14 ♕g4 ♕b6 is more unclear, though still roughly balanced) 14 exf6 gxf6 15 ♕g4 can lead to a draw after 15...fxg5 16 ♕xg5+, with perpetual check, or 15...f5 16 ♕g3 f4 17 ♗xf4 ♘f5 18 ♕g4 ♘h6 19 ♕g3 ♘f5 with a repetition.

25) No, because 10 ♗xh7+? ♔xh7 11 ♘g5+ ♔h6! leaves Black a piece up. After 12 ♕c2 g6 13 ♘xe6 fxe6 14 h5 Black has various ways to hang on, but the most accurate defence is 14...♖g8! 15 hxg6+ ♗h4!.

26) 13 ♗xh7+!? is good but complex: 13...♔xh7 14 ♘g5+ ♔g6 and both 15 h4 and 15 b5 give White an open-ended attack that should provide him with a large advantage. White might consider preparing the sacrifice with 13 b5!; e.g., 13...♘e7 14 ♗xh7+ ♔xh7 15 ♘g5+ ♔g6 16 ♕g4 or 13...♘a5 14 ♗xh7+ ♔xh7 15 ♘g5+ ♔g6 16 h4 intending h5+.

27) 10 ♗xh7+?! leads to unclear play. The critical defence is 10...♔xh7 11 ♘g5+ ♔g6!, when 12 ♕d3+ f5 13 exf6+ ♔xf6 lets the king run, while 12 b4 ♘dxe5 (12...♗e7? 13 ♕d3+ is now more of a problem) 13 ♕c2+ (13 bxc5 ♕a6) 13...f5 14 bxc5 ♕b5 is just a mess. Since White has a good game with normal moves such as 10 ♘bd2, the sacrifice is objectively un-justified, though in practice it may still prove effective since players often blunder when under attack.

28) 12 ♗xh7+! is best, but should only draw. After 12...♔xh7 13 ♕h5+ ♔g8 14 ♕xf7+ ♔h7 White has no more than perpetual check. Instead 12...♔h8?? loses to 13 ♕h5, while one game featured 12...♔f8??, which was presumably an extremely unwise winning attempt! After 13 ♕h5! g6 (13...♕xh1+ 14 ♔e2 ♗a6+ 15 ♗d3) 14 ♗xg6! ♗f6 (14...fxg6 15 ♕h8#; 14...♕xh1+ 15 ♔e2 ♗a6+ 16 ♗d3) 15 ♗e4 Black had seen enough and resigned.

29) 11 ♗xh7+ leads to an unclear game. Whether to choose it is a matter of taste, since the play is otherwise roughly equal with little chance for Black to go badly wrong. After 11...♔xh7 12 ♘g5+, 12...♔h6! is essential – White has no dark-squared bishop, so h6 is safer than usual. 13 ♘de4 (not 13 ♕c2? g6) intending ♕d2 gives White play for the piece, but Black can scramble; e.g., 13...g6 14 h5 ♔g7 or 13...♗e7 14 ♕d2 ♕e8 15 0-0-0 f6.

30) 11 ♗xh7+! is good here for a surprising reason: it helps White trap the black queen: 11...♔xh7 12 ♘g5+ ♔g6 (12...♔g8 is also met with 13 ♕d3! followed by ♖fb1, but not 13 ♕h5?? ♕xc2) 13 ♕d3+ f5 14 exf6+ ♔xf6 15 ♖fb1 and the queen is lost since 15...♘b4 16 ♕e2 ♕xc2 17 ♕xe6# is mate!

MATE

10 Advanced Exercises

This chapter features the most difficult exercises in this book. The themes are similar to those from the earlier chapters, but they are much harder to solve for various reasons. The ideas may be less standard, or there may be a strong defensive idea to overcome, and traps to avoid. Generally, you will need to see more deeply into the positions.

Don't worry if you can't solve these exercises! Either come back to them later, or else try your best, and learn from the solutions. It is important to appreciate that chess can be a complicated game. At the board you will sometimes get positions where you can't work out the best move, and need to make the best guess you can. When comparing your answers with the solutions, you can be proud if you just got the first move right, even if you were unsure about the follow-up. In a real game, your only task – *ever!* – is to play a good move in the current position.

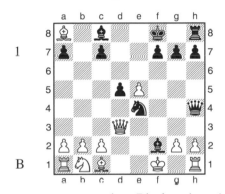

An accurate move gives Black a nice win in this game from a German junior event.

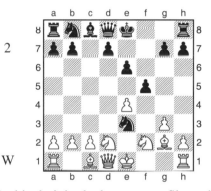

Black's knight looks strong. Show how White ignores it and gets a winning attack.

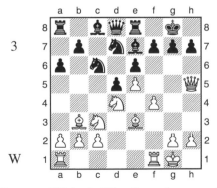

How can White brilliantly make use of his development advantage?

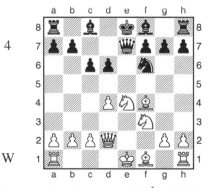

Take a look at the move 10 ♗xd6. What is the idea, and why doesn't it work?

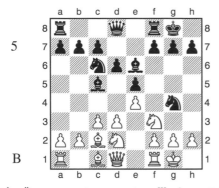

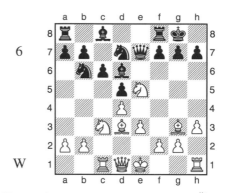

"♗+♘ are worth more than ♖+♙, so Black shouldn't take on f2." True or false?

Choose between exchanging by 13 ♘xd7 or supporting the knight with 13 f4.

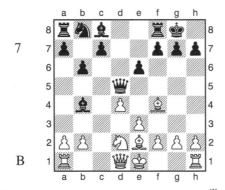

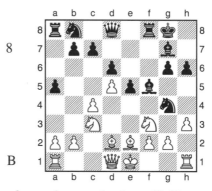

Black decided to grab a pawn by 10...♕xg2. Was this a good idea?

Go forward or go backward? Choose between 12...♘xf2 and 12...♘f6.

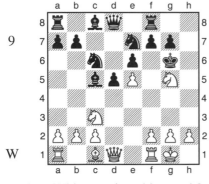

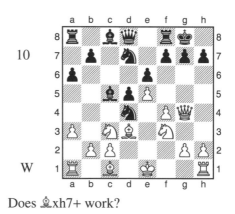

How does White continue his attack?

Does ♗xh7+ work?

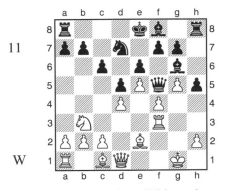

11

W

A tricky sequence gives White a huge advantage.

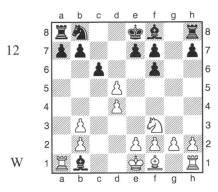

12

W

Do you see a familiar opening tactic? But does it work here?

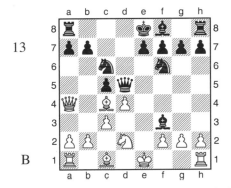

13

B

The silliest-looking move on the board gives Black a big advantage!

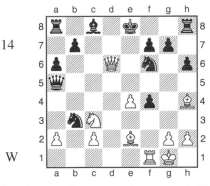

14

W

Time is more important than material here.

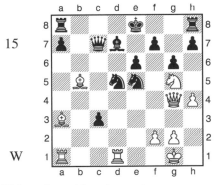

15

W

White wins with a dramatic move.

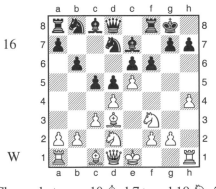

16

W

Choose between 10 ♗xh7+ and 10 ♘g5.

Solutions to Advanced Exercises

1) 12...Bd4!! (threatening mate on f2; 12...Nc5?! is parried by 13 Bg5! Qxg5 14 Qxd5, while 12...Bc5? is no good because after 13 Be3 there's no follow-up: 13...Ba6 14 Qxa6 Bxe3 15 Qc8+, etc.) 13 Be3 (or: 13 Qa3+ Bc5; 13 Qf3 Ba6+; 13 g3 Qh3+ 14 Ke1 Bf2+ and ....Bg4+) 13...Nc5! (...Ba6 is coming one way or another) 14 Qd2 (14 Qxd4 Ba6+) 14...Ba6+ 15 Kg1 Qf4! (a beautiful double pin) 16 Bf2 Bxf2+! 17 Qxf2 Qc1+ and mate next move.

2) 9 Qh5+! g6 (9...Kf8 10 Nc4 Nxc2+ 11 Kd1 Nxa1 12 Nd6 Qe7 13 e5 and Bg5) 10 Qh6! Nxc2+ (10...Nxg2+ 11 Kf1 traps the knight) 11 Kd1 Nxa1 12 Nc4 and with Nd6+ and/or Bg5 coming, White is completely winning; e.g., 12...d5 (12...Qe7 13 Bf4) 13 exd5 Qf6 14 b3 and Bb2. From the diagram position, 9 Qf3? Nxc2+ 10 Kd1 Nxa1 11 Qh5+ g6 12 Qh6 Qc7 and 9 Qe2? f4!? are far less clear.

3) With a sacrificial mating attack: 13 Nxd5! exd5 14 Qxf7+!! Kxf7 15 Bxd5+ Kg6 (15...Kf8 16 Ne6+ is hopeless for Black) 16 f5+ Kh5 17 Bf3+ Kh4 and White has various ways to mate, including 18 g3+ Kh3 19 Bg2+ Kg4 20 Rf4+ Kh5 21 Bf3+ Kh6 22 Rh4#.

4) 10 Bxd6?? has the point that after 10...Qxe4+ 11 Kf2 White intends Re1, pinning the black queen. It doesn't work because after 11...Bxd6! 12 Re1 0-0 13 Rxe4 Nxe4+ the knight fork wins back the queen, keeping an extra rook.

5) This was a trick question. B+N are indeed worth more than R+P, but 9...Bxf2+! is a very good move because after 10 Rxf2 Black isn't taking the rook but instead playing 10...Ne3!, forking Q+B. The final critical point is that 11 Qe2 Nxc2 12 Rb1 Ba2! traps the rook, so Black emerges material up. One game continued 13 b3 Bxb1 14 Nxb1 Na1! 15 Qa2 Nxb3 16 Qxb3 and White soon resigned because R+3P are definitely more valuable than B+N!

6) 13 f4? f6 gives White a serious problem on the e-file, made worse by the loose bishop on g3. 14 Ng4 (14 Nxd7 Qxe3+ 15 Ne2 Bxd7 gives Black a strong extra pawn) 14...h5 and now 15 Nf2 Qxe3+ 16 Ne2 is miserable for White, while 15 Qf3 hxg4 16 hxg4 doesn't give him enough for the piece. If you rejected 13 Nxd7! because you thought it failed to 13...Bxg3?, then you missed a further intermezzo: 14 Bxh7+! Kxh7 (14...Kh8 15 Qh5 Qxe3+ 16 Kd1) 15 Nxf8+ Kg8 16 fxg3 Qxe3+ 17 Ne2 with a material advantage.

7) 10...Qxg2? loses because White gets the better of the tactical dogfight. But it's a close-run thing, and one should not assume that such pawns are poisoned – it all depends on the specifics. 11 Bf3! Bxd2+ 12 Kxd2! (12 Ke2? Qh3! lets Black mostly off the hook) 12...Qxf2+ 13 Kc3! (after 13 Kc1? c6 the game is very much alive, since 14 h4 Ba6 throws the queen a lifeline: 15 Rh2 Qf1) and now 13...c6 is met by the easily-missed 14 h4!, when there is no good answer to the threat of Rh2. Black's best try, 13...e5, is most convincingly answered with 14 Rf1 (14 dxe5?! b5! 15 Bxa8 b4+ 16 Kb3 Na6 is at least messy) 14...Qh4 15 Bg3 and Bxa8.

8) 12...Nf6?! is the move you'd have to choose if you didn't think the sacrifice worked, but White has the better game after 13 g4 followed by g5, gaining squares on the kingside; e.g., 13...Be4 14 g5 hxg5 15 Bxg5. But the resolute 12...Nxf2! gives Black strong play after 13 Kxf2 e4! (a thematic move, unleashing the bishop on g7) 14 g4 (14 Nxe4 Bxe4 favours

114

Black, while 14 ♘h2? ♗d4+!? 15 ♔f1 ♕h4 16 ♕e1 ♕xh3! is a decisive attack) 14...exf3 15 ♗xf3 ♗d3! and with material now level, Black has far better pieces and a big advantage.

9) 11 ♘e2! brings essential reserves into play: 11...♘xe5 (or 11...♖h8 12 ♘f4+ ♔xg5 13 ♘h5+) 12 ♘f4+! ♔f5!? (12...♔xg5? 13 ♕h5+ ♔f6 14 ♕h4+ and now 14...g5 15 ♘h5+ or 14...♔f5 15 ♘h5 with mate to follow) allows White a number of ways to win, though none of them are trivial; e.g., 13 ♘h7 g6 14 ♘h3 (threatening g4+) 14...g5 15 ♕h5.

10) 11 ♗xh7+ works tactically, but leads to unclear play. This is because White is sacrificing so much material that Black can give up his queen to avoid mate: 11...♔xh7! 12 ♘g5+ ♔g8 13 ♕h5 ♕xg5! 14 ♕xg5 ♘xc2+ 15 ♔d1 ♘xa1 gives Black a lot of pieces for the queen, while White lacks the firepower to force mate any time soon.

11) 14 h3! (by covering the g4-square, White threatens ♗d3) 14...♕xc2 15 ♕f1! (threatening 16 ♖c3 ♕e4 17 ♗d3) 15...♘h7 (15...♗b4 16 a3) 16 ♖c3 ♕g6 17 ♗d3 f5 18 exf6 ♕f7 and Black has rescued his queen, but his position has been wrecked in the process. After 19 ♗xh7 ♖xh7 20 f5 exf5 21 ♕e2+ ♔d8 22 ♘a5 ♘b6 23 ♘xb7+ ♕xb7 24 g6 ♖h8 25 ♗g5, for instance, Black can resign.

12) Your task here was to reject the tempting 9 dxc6??. With 9...♗e4! Black defends against cxb7 and is a piece up. The problem for White is that after 10 ♖xa7 ♖xa7 11 c7 Black can stop the pawn from promoting with 11...♖a1+ 12 ♔d2 ♗h6+! 13 e3 0-0. So 9 ♖xb1 is necessary, with a roughly equal game.

13) Let's first see why ordinary moves fail: 8...♕d7? 9 ♘xf3 is fairly good for White, while 8...♘g5? 9 ♘xf3! ♕xg2 10 ♔e2! gives White a big development advantage. With 8...♗d1!! Black counters the attack on his queen by hitting the white queen, and opens the diagonal to allow for ...♕xg2 next move. After 9 ♕xd1 (9 ♗xd5?? ♗xa4 leaves Black a piece up, while 9 ♔xd1 ♕xg2 gives Black an extra pawn and a great position) 9...♕xg2, White has no development advantage to make up for his missing pawn and shattered position. Then 10 ♕f3 (10 ♖f1 e6 is also miserable for White) 10...♕xf3 11 ♘xf3 is an ending Black should win.

14) 17 ♗b5+! has the idea of preventing ...♕c5+. After 17...axb5 (17...♗d7? allows 18 ♗xd7+ ♘xd7 19 ♕e7#) 18 ♗xf6 gxf6 19 ♘d5 ♕d8 20 ♘xf6+ (not 20 ♘c7+? ♕xc7 21 ♕xc7 ♘d4) 20...♕xf6 21 ♕xf6 Black loses his knight.

15) 21 ♘xe6! ♕b7 (21...fxe6 22 ♕xe6+ ♔d8 23 ♖xd5 gives White a decisive attack, while 21...♘xg4 loses to 22 ♘xc7+ ♕xc7 23 ♗xd7+ ♔d8 24 ♗xg4+) 22 ♗xd7+ ♕xd7 (22...♔xd7 23 ♘c5++; 22...♘xd7 23 ♖xd5 ♕xd5 24 ♘c7+) 23 ♘g7+ ♔d8 24 ♕e4 leads to a rout. Other moves in the diagram position don't work for White: after 21 ♗xd7+? ♕xd7 he has merely sufficient compensation: 22 ♕e4 (22 ♕d4 f6) 22...♘c6 23 ♕e2 and ♘e4. And 21 ♕h3? ♗xb5 22 ♘xe6 fxe6 23 ♕xe6+ ♘e7 24 ♗d6 only leaves the question of how much better Black is.

16) 10 ♗xh7+? offers White little: 10...♔xh7 11 ♘g5+ ♔g8! 12 ♕h5 fxg5 13 hxg5 and now 13...♖f5! holds since the black queen is defended (unlike Exercise 22 in Chapter 9) and White can't do much more than give checks. On the other hand, 10 ♘g5! is strong: 10...fxg5 (with h7 and e6 attacked, there's little choice) and *now* 11 ♗xh7+! forces mate: 11...♔xh7 12 hxg5+ ♔g8 (or 12...♔g6 13 ♕h5+ ♔f5 14 ♕h7+ g6 15 ♕h3+ ♔f4 16 g3+ ♔xg5 17 ♘f3#) 13 ♖h8+! (as the queen isn't blocking the rook!) 13...♔xh8 14 ♕h5+ ♔g8 15 g6, mating.

11 Tests

This series of seven tests helps you judge how well you handle opening tactics. The themes are similar to ones we have seen in earlier chapters of the book, but you are given far fewer clues about what to look for. The number of asterisks shows the level from easy (*) to very difficult (*****). For the first four tests, there is a rough hint as to the ideas involved, but for the final three you are completely on your own. Tests 6 and 7 are called 'Stop Press!' because they feature positions from the couple of months before this book went to the printers.

I suggest writing your answer down once you have carefully decided what you would play. Don't just instantly choose a move and then look at the answer. That doesn't work at the board in a real game! The solutions start on page 123. You only need to have seen up to the moment where I award points. Add up your scores and once you have finished all the tests, look at the table on page 126.

Test 1: Mate

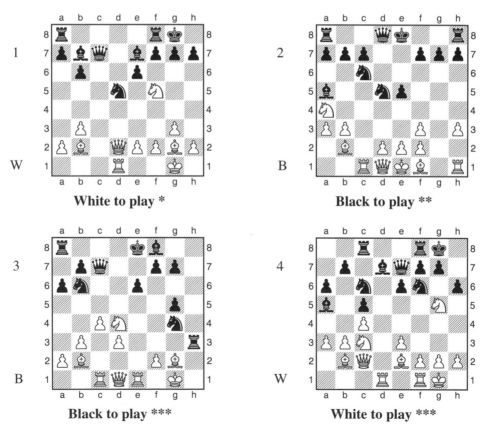

White to play *

Black to play **

Black to play ***

White to play ***

116

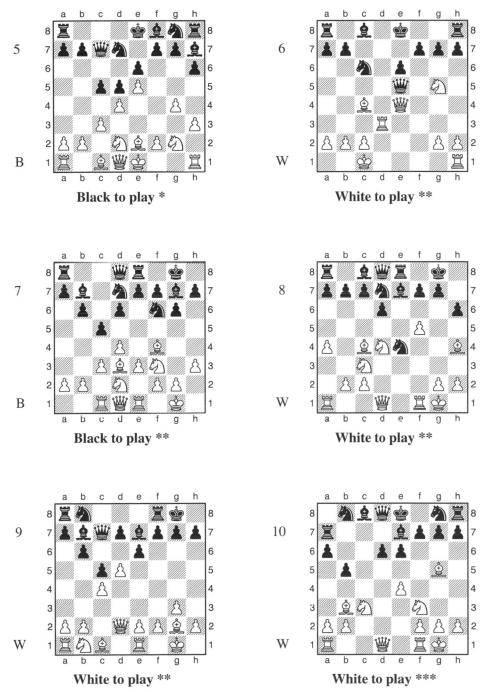

5 — Black to play *

6 — White to play **

7 — Black to play **

8 — White to play **

9 — White to play **

10 — White to play ***

Test 3: More Trapped Pieces

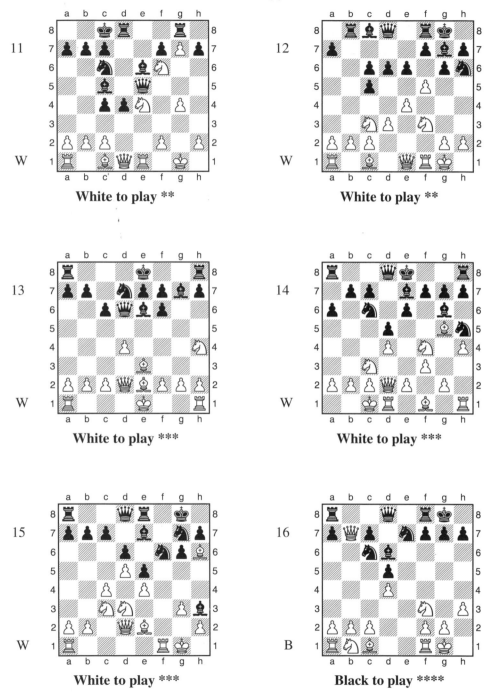

11   **White to play** **

12   **White to play** **

13   **White to play** ***

14   **White to play** ***

15   **White to play** ***

16   **Black to play** ****

Test 4: General Tactics

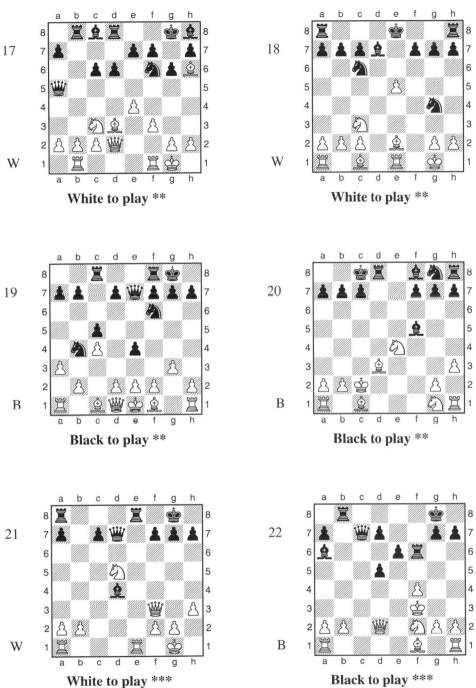

17   White to play **

18   White to play **

19   Black to play **

20   Black to play **

21   White to play ***

22   Black to play ***

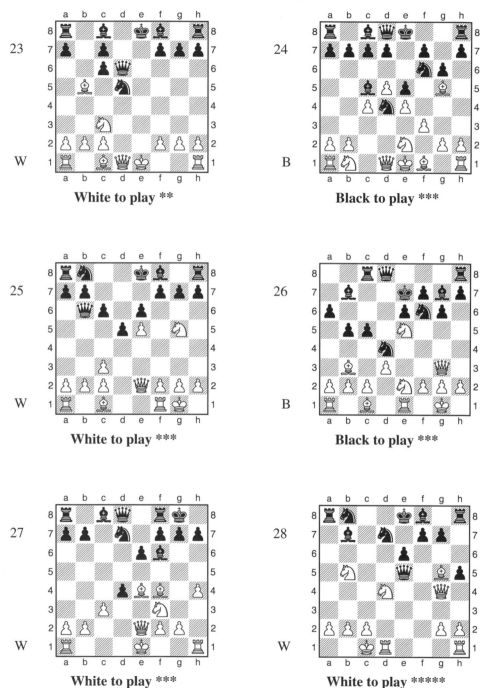

23 White to play **

24 Black to play ***

25 White to play ***

26 Black to play ***

27 White to play ***

28 White to play *****

Test 6: Stop Press! 1

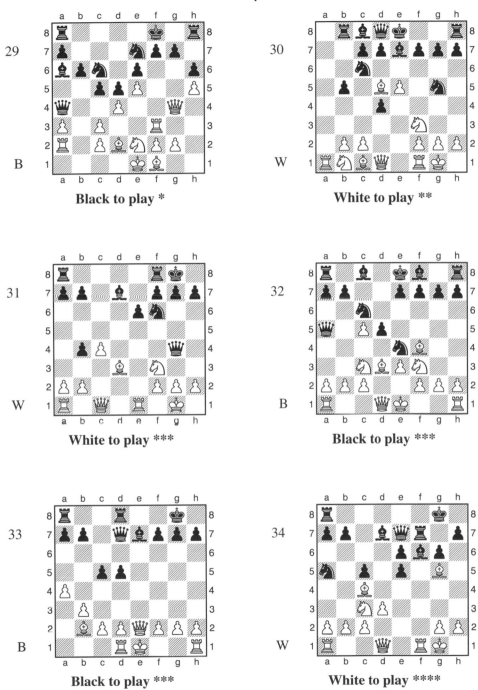

29   B

Black to play *

30

White to play **

31   W

White to play ***

32   B

Black to play ***

33   B

Black to play ***

34   W

White to play ****

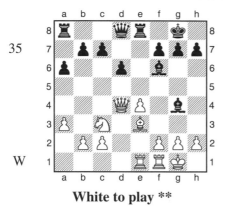

35

White to play **

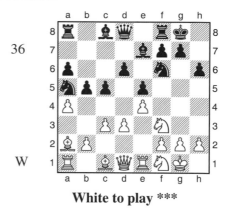

36

White to play ***

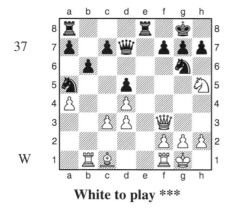

37

White to play ***

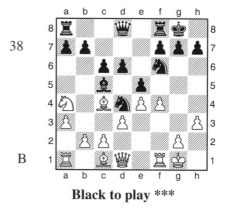

38

Black to play ***

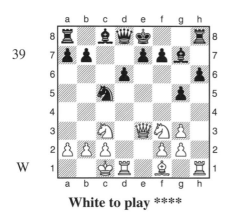

39

White to play ****

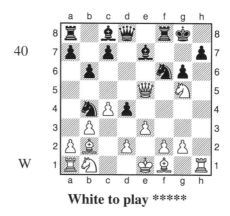

40

White to play *****

Solutions for Tests

Test 1

1) White had a decisive blow up his sleeve: 19 ♕h6! (*1 point*) 19...gxh6 (19...♗f6 20 ♗xf6 changes nothing) 20 ♘xh6# is a standard mate pattern.

2) Black wins with a sudden stab to the heart: 11...♘e3! (*2 points*) wins the white queen thanks to the pin on the d2-pawn and the fact that 12 fxe3 allows 12...♕h4#.

3) Black wins the game in dramatic fashion: 18...♖h1+! (*3 points*) is both a decoy and a deflection. The clever point is that after 19 ♗xh1 (19 ♔xh1 allows 19...♕h2#) 19...♕h2+ 20 ♔f1 the bishop standing on h1 instead of g2 allows Black to play 20...♕xf2#. Instead 18...♕h2+? 19 ♔f1 leaves Black with no effective follow-up.

4) We've seen this theme before: 15 ♘d5! (*3 points*) is the modified Siberian Trap, with the bishop playing the key role after 15...exd5 16 ♗xf6 ♕xf6 17 ♕h7#.

Test 2

5) Black has something far better than simply developing: 11...cxd4! wins a couple of pawns since 12 cxd4? is impossible due to 12...♗c2! (*1 point*), trapping the queen.

6) White wins with a standard tactic: 15 ♖d8+! (*2 points*) is a typical decoy idea, with additional elements of a deflection and a skewer. 15...♔e7 leaves the h8-rook to be taken, 15...♔xd8 16 ♘xf7+ costs Black his queen as the king has been decoyed into a knight fork, while 15...♘xd8 16 ♕xe5 exploits the deflection of the black knight.

7) Black wins a piece with the pawn fork 11...e5! (*2 points*), followed by ...e4 after the bishop moves.

8) Black has just grabbed a pawn on e4, but White replies with a tactic of his own: 13 ♗xf7+! ♔xf7 14 ♘e6 (*2 points*) traps and wins the black queen.

9) One good move brings Black's position crashing down: 11 d6! (*2 points*) forks queen and bishop, and either capture loses a bishop: 11...♗xd6 (11...♕xd6 12 ♗xb7) 12 ♗xb7 (overloading the queen) 12...♕xb7 13 ♕xd6.

10) In the opening we sometimes get a fleeting chance for a double attack. 10 ♕d4! (*3 points*) attacks both the rook on a7 and the g7-pawn. After 10...♘c6 (10...♖d7 11 ♕xg7 ♗f6 12 ♕xh8 ♗xh8 13 ♗xd8 is similar) 11 ♕xg7 ♗f6 (even worse is 11...♗xg5 12 ♕xh8) 12 ♕xh8 ♗xh8 13 ♗xd8 ♔xd8 Black has only a bishop for a rook.

Test 3

11) White traps the black queen mid-board: 16 f4! d3+ 17 ♔g2 ♕d4 18 c3! (*2 points*).

12) White wins material with 11 f6! (*2 points*). Then 11...♗h8 12 ♗xh6 and 11...♗xf6 12 ♗xh6 both cost Black his knight, while 11...♕xf6 12 ♗g5 leaves his queen trapped.

13) Black has boxed his queen in. White takes advantage with 11 ♗f4! ♕d5 12 c4 ♕e4 13 f3 (*3 points*), when the queen is trapped in the middle of the board.

14) White wins a piece: after a couple of piece exchanges, namely 10 ♗xe7 ♕xe7 11 ♘xh5 ♗xh5, his pawns do the trick: 12 g4 ♗g6 13 h5 (*3 points*), trapping the bishop.

15) White wins material by 17 ♖xf6! ♗xf6 18 g4 (*3 points*), trapping the h3-bishop.

16) Black wins with 11...♘b4!, threatening ...♘xc2. While this threat is easy to parry, after 12 ♘a3 a6! (*4 points*) we see the real idea: the white queen is trapped. After 13 ♘e5 ♖b8 14 ♕a7 ♖b6! Black brings a knight to c6 and it's goodnight to the queen.

Test 4

17) White wins with an odd twist on a standard theme. 14 ♘d5! is an idea we have seen before, threatening both ♘xe7# and ♕xa5. It seems like the check 14...♕c5+ might save Black, but then comes 15 ♗e3 (*2 points*), trapping the queen.

18) White wins a piece: 14 e6! (*2 points*) breaks the bishop's defence of the g4-knight because of the pin on the e-file after 14...♗xe6 15 ♗xg4.

19) Black's knight does not have to retreat because 11...♘d3+! (*2 points*) forces open the e-file and wins. 12 exd3 exd3+ 13 ♗e2 ♖fe8! (13...dxe2? 14 ♕xe2 squanders Black's advantage) is a disaster for White, who can't even castle without losing a whole rook.

20) Black wins material thanks to a pin: 14...♖xd3! 15 ♔xd3 ♘f6 (*2 points*) is a standard theme, sacrificing an exchange to create a powerful pin. Black emerges with a bishop and two good pawns for a rook – a small material advantage – and excellent winning chances due to White's exposed king and poor development.

21) It looks like Black has survived the opening, but White has a devastating move that shows otherwise: 17 ♖e7!! (*3 points*) cuts off the queen's guard of f7, and Black's loose rook on a8 proves fatal after 17...♖xe7 18 ♘xe7+ ♕xe7 19 ♕xa8+. 17...♕c6 18 ♖xe8+! ♖xe8 19 ♘e7+ costs Black his queen, while 17...♕b5 is met by 18 ♘xc7!, forking everything (this is far clearer than 18 ♕xf7+?! ♔h8).

22) With White's king his furthest advanced piece, it should be no surprise that Black has a devastating move here. 17...♖xb2! (*3 points*) wins. The main point is 18 ♕xb2 ♕xf4#, and 18 ♕d4 ♖xf4+ 19 ♕xf4 ♖xf2+ costs White his queen, while 18 ♖c1 is also met by 18...♖xf4+.

Test 5

23) 9 ♕xd5! (*2 points*) uses a double pin to win a piece. The bishop pins the pawn against the king, and the queen pins it against the rook on a8: 9...♕xd5 (9...cxd5 is illegal; 9...cxb5 10 ♕xa8 grabs the rook) 10 ♘xd5 ♔d7 (10...cxb5 11 ♘xc7+ followed by ♘xa8 makes a decisive material gain) 11 ♗a4 and White keeps an extra knight.

24) The pin on Black's f6-knight looks like a problem until you see 7...♘xe4! (*3 points*). This is an explosive breaking of the pin, turning it into a *battery*. 8 ♗xd8 allows mate by 8...♘xf3+ 9 gxf3 ♗f2#, while 8 fxe4 ♕xg5 leaves Black a solid pawn up. 8 ♕xd4 is best met by 8...♗xd4! 9 ♗xd8 ♗xb2 10 ♗xc7 (10 fxe4 ♔xd8) 10...♘c5!, winning material.

25) Black's position appears solid, but 10 ♕h5! (*3 points*) shows that this is an illusion. There's no good way to defend f7 and e6 (which is threatened thanks to the pin on the f7-pawn). 10...g6 (10...♕c7 11 ♘xe6) 11 ♕f3 ♕c7 12 ♕f6 ♖g8 13 ♘xe6! (exploiting the loose rook on g8; 13 ♘xh7? ♘d7 is far from clear) 13...♕d7 (13...fxe6 14 ♕xe6+ and ♕xg8) 14 ♘xf8 ♖xf8 15 ♗h6! ♖g8 16 e6 and Black is busted: 16...fxe6 17 ♖fe1.

26) The fact that White hasn't connected his rooks allows Black a deadly blow: 15...♘xe2+! 16 ♖xe2 c4! (*3 points*) and the bishop is trapped because 17 dxc4 allows a back-rank mate with

17...♕d1+. Back-rank mate isn't usually an opening theme, but with the white queen absent and the queen's bishop still on the first rank, it happened here.

27) The standard sacrifice works here: 12 ♗xh7+! ♔xh7 13 ♘g5+ (*3 points*) and Black will be mated quickly: 13...♔g6 14 ♕e4+, 13...♗xg5 14 hxg5+ ♔g6 15 ♕h5+ ♔f5 16 g6+ or 13...♔g8 14 ♕h5 ♗xg5 15 hxg5 f6 16 g6.

28) White has a forcing path to victory, but must be ready to sacrifice heavily: 15 ♘c7+! ♕xc7 16 ♘xe6! ♕e5 (any other queen move is answered in the same way, while Black is mated directly after 16...fxe6 17 ♕xe6+ ♗e7 18 ♕xe7# or 16...hxg4 17 ♘xc7#) 17 ♘c7+! (*5 points*) 17...♕xc7 and now we have the position we saw in Exercise 23 of Chapter 2.

Test 6

29) 14...♘xe5! (*1 point*) exploits the pin along the 4th rank to fork White's queen and rook.

30) White wins with a double attack: 12 ♘xg5! ♗xg5 13 ♕h5! (*2 points*) threatens both ♕xf7# and ♕xg5.

31) 16 ♖e5! (*3 points*) traps the queen by cutting off its safe retreats. There's no answer to the threats of both ♖g5 and h3.

32) The preliminary exchange 7...♘xc3 (not 7...e5?? 8 ♗xe4) 8 bxc3 lays the ground for a winning pawn fork or queen fork: 8...e5! (*3 points*) and if the f4-bishop saves its skin, 9...e4 wins one of White's other minor pieces, while after 9 ♘xe5 ♕xc3+ or 9 ♗xe5 ♘xe5 10 ♘xe5 ♕xc3+ it is the queen that delivers the fork.

33) White's failure to castle allows Black to win material with 14...♖e8!. Even though White can avoid a pin on the queen by playing 15 0-0, there is still a discovered attack, and 15...♗f6 (*3 points*) picks off the *loose piece* on b2.

34) 16 ♖xf6! is a typical way to remove an enemy bishop and replace it with a piece that is more effectively pinned: 16...♖xf6 17 ♘e4 (*4 points*) 17...♖af8 and Black has no way to break the pin before White strengthens it further; e.g., 18 ♕e1 ♘xc4 (18...♘c6 19 ♕e3) 19 dxc4 ♔g7 20 ♘xf6 ♖xf6 21 ♕xe5.

Test 7

35) 14 e5! (*2 points*) is a double attack on the black bishops, winning one of them.

36) White uses a theme from *Chess Opening Traps for Kids*, the pinned knight on the rook's file, to set up a discovered attack: 14 axb5! axb5 15 b4! ♘c6 16 ♗xf7+ (*3 points*) 16...♖xf7 17 ♖xa8 with a decisive material advantage.

37) 16 ♗h6! (*3 points*) destroys Black's kingside because 16...gxh6 allows the knight fork 17 ♘f6+. Also hopeless for Black is 16...♘h4 17 ♕g3 ♘f5 18 ♘f6+ ♔h8 19 ♗xg7+!.

38) The double check 12...♘e2++! wins thanks to a mating idea: 13 ♔h2 (13 ♔h1 avoids mate but loses material to the knight fork 13...♘g3+) 13...♘g4+! (*3 points*) and Black mates next move: 14 ♔h1 ♘g3# or 14 hxg4 ♕h4#. Black must avoid 12...♘xc2+?, which seeks material gain, but fails because after 13 ♘xc5 ♘xa1 White has 14 fxe5! dxe5 15 ♗e3, staying ahead on material.

39) 14 ♗b5+! wins because of two pins (*4 points*). After 14...♔f8 15 ♕xc5 the d-file pin against the queen costs Black a piece (then 15...♕a5 16 ♕e3 ♗xc3 doesn't save Black because

17 ♕xc3 hits the rook on h8). And 14...♗d7 15 ♖xd6 uses the pin on the e-file and leaves Black hopelessly bound: 15...♖c8 (15...♔f8 16 ♕xc5) 16 ♗xd7+ ♘xd7 17 ♖hd1 ♖c7 18 ♘b5. Also 14...♘d7 15 ♖xd6 ♔f8 16 ♖d3 is no good for Black because even if he evacuates both pieces with 16...♖c7 17 ♖hd1 ♘f6, the back-rank check 18 ♖d8+ wins.

40) 13 c5! (*5 points*) opens a square for the bishop on c4, and this is enough to create a winning attack on the exposed black king. After 13...bxc5?! 14 ♖xh7! White wins since 14...♘xh7 15 ♗c4+ is devastating. And 13...h5 14 ♗xd4 ♘c2+ (14...bxc5 15 ♗c4+ ♔g7 16 ♗b2 and White dominates the board) 15 ♔d1 ♘xa1 (or 15...♘xd4 16 ♗c4+ ♔g7 17 exd4 with extra pawns) 16 ♗c4+ ♔g7 17 ♗xa1 leaves Black hopelessly pinned; e.g., 17...bxc5 18 ♕e4 ♖b8 19 ♖xh5!.

Score-Table

Test number	Maximum score	Your score
1	9	
2	12	
3	17	
4	14	
5	19	
6	16	
7	20	
Total	107	

Rate your score:

0-20	Revision necessary!
21-40	Focus on your weaker areas
41-60	Shows potential
61-80	Promising talent
81-90	Potential international player
91-95	Potential master strength
96-107	Potential (or actual!) grandmaster

HUNTING THE KING

Further Improvement

Is it really that time again? Yes, we have reached the end of the book, but there are many adventures in the opening ahead. Firstly, play lots of games. This is by far the best way to improve all aspects of your chess. Take the games seriously, and study them afterwards to understand what went well and what went wrong.

If you are looking for further books to help you study chess openings, you are in luck, because more books are published on openings than any other phase of the game. Most of them are specialized, and aimed at high-level players, but there are plenty of general instructional ones too. If you haven't already got them, there are two other books in the 'Chess for Kids' series:

Chess Openings for Kids (Watson and Burgess) discusses 50 major openings, giving their main variations and explaining the strategies behind them as well as some of the key tactics.

Chess Opening Traps for Kids (Burgess) examines 100 tactical themes that can lead to a quick win (or loss!) in the openings.

Two other general guides can be recommended:

Fundamental Chess Openings (Van der Sterren) is a large book that covers all openings. It is full of explanations in words with relatively few complex variations or analysis. It will help you choose which openings might appeal to you.

Understanding the Chess Openings (Collins) also describes all the major openings but is more selective in its approach, focusing on structures and common strategic themes.

Otherwise, if you particularly enjoyed Chapter 9 of this book, then *Essential Chess Sacrifices* (LeMoir) goes into detail about a number of other standard sacrifices. And if you are really ambitious, then John Watson's four-volume series *Mastering the Chess Openings* is a treasure trove of opening ideas. Start with Volume 1 and its first three chapters. This volume also covers the 1 e4 e5 openings that you'll get a lot in junior and club chess.

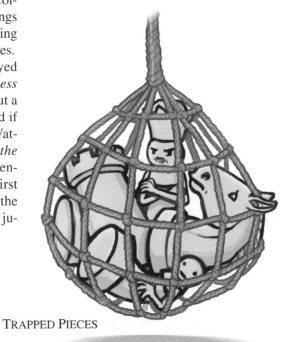

TRAPPED PIECES

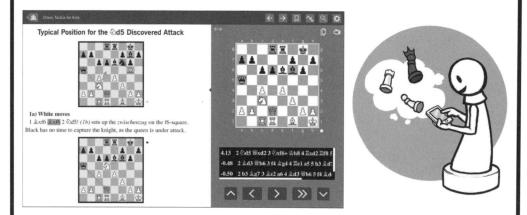